LIKE
NOTHING

ON EARTH

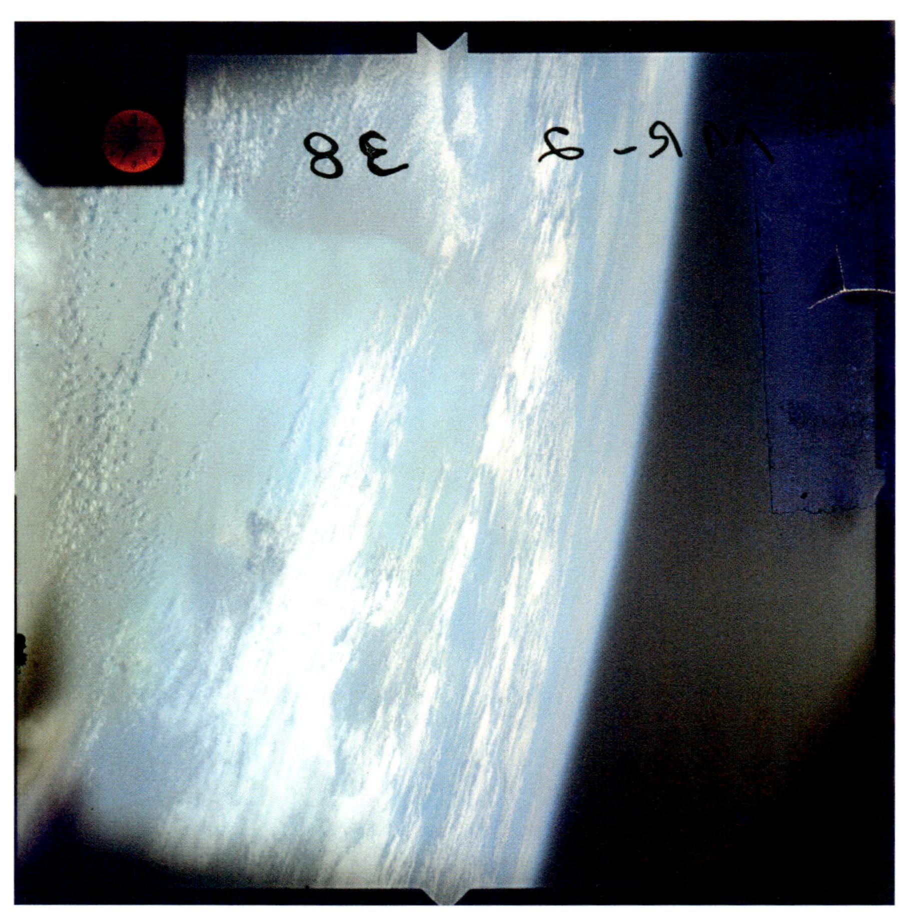
MR-2
38

Like Nothing on Earth: Photographic Artifacts from Early NASA Missions

Paul Morgan

Current Editions

Introduction

When Alan Shepard and Gus Grissom became the first Americans to enter outer space in 1961, they carried no handheld cameras. Instead, the capsules they rode in were equipped with automated photographic systems designed to document their flights. At the time, NASA treated these early Project Mercury missions as engineering trials.

Fixed-perspective J.A. Maurer 220G 70mm cameras produced time-lapse sequences of stills. Every six seconds, the shutter opened autonomously, capturing whatever lay beyond the module's small window. A stopwatch was automatically burned into each frame. Once developed, engineers annotated the GAF Super Anscochrome film with technical data, permanently altering these early visual records of space.

NASA's utilitarian method of documentation mirrored the U.S. government's broader view of space—not as a frontier for discovery, but as a proving ground for Cold War technology. The same launch systems that carried astronauts into orbit also installed reconnaissance satellites. Rockets powerful enough to deliver instruments to the Moon could easily carry nuclear warheads across continents. Every successful space launch doubled as propaganda for missile technology. Whether or not the American public understood, military agendas pressed forward.

In May 1961, after the third Mercury flight, President Kennedy urged Congress to commit to landing a human on the Moon within nine years. It was an almost unimaginable request—only two astronauts had reached suborbital space, and no NASA mission had yet orbited the Earth, much less the Moon. The technological demands, both in time and money, were staggering.

But NASA understood something many state actors do: narratives shape public opinion. It was one thing to argue the military-industrial complex needs more powerful rockets. It was another to capture that demand in heroic images of astronauts, moonwalks, and Earth seen from afar.

Fixed-position cameras alone couldn't deliver the emotional force required. The emerging story needed movement, presence, and spectacle—the kind of visuals only achievable with human involvement in the act of photographing. NASA realized the Mercury, Gemini, and Apollo missions had to be seen through the eyes of the astronauts themselves.

Nine months after Kennedy's address, John Glenn carried an Ansco Autoset 35mm camera, purchased at a Cocoa Beach, Florida drug store, aboard his Friendship 7 capsule. With it, he shot the first human-captured, still photograph of Earth. Over the course of three orbits, he shot 75 frames of film—many out of focus, filled with glare, or blotched with light leaks. The difficulties of space photography were real.

For the next decade, every NASA mission included handheld film cameras for astronauts to use—often several. But it was not an artistic free-for-all inside and outside the capsule. Like every other part of the missions, documenting space was guided by detailed checklists—what to shoot, when, and on which film. This led to amusing moments—when William Anders stood on the Moon framing what would become the iconic *Earthrise* image, Frank Borman joked, "Hey, don't take that, it's not scheduled."

Between 1961 and 1972, NASA astronauts shot over 25,000 photographs. The collection contains many iconic images: *Blue Marble, Earthrise, Bootprint*. But what drew me to this archive was the mistakes; the flubs between these iconic scenes.

Missions frequently used color reversal film, which had a fragile photosensitive layer prone to inconsistency. Images were often affected by light leaks, radiation artifacts, and color streaks. Spacesuits significantly reduced astronauts' dexterity, making it difficult to adjust focus or shutter speed. To compensate, they used techniques like Zone Focusing and Sunny 16, which sometimes produced beautifully wrong

exposures when transitioning between scenes. And with only a finite number of frames per roll, majestic views of space were often cut off as the film ran out.

The 55 photographs in *Like Nothing on Earth* serve as a reflection on human agency. Through NASA, the U.S. government spent billions of dollars to develop increasingly advanced and powerful weaponry. But to sell this trajectory to the public, they needed a compelling story—*Progress Into Space*. By placing cameras in astronauts' hands, NASA introduced subjectivity, creativity, and personal judgment into the storytelling. The astronauts believed in The Mission, taking images that promoted its goals.

And yet, once human hands entered the frame, so did unpredictability. Despite every checklist and control, the archive reveals moments where slippages occur. Narratives might be engineered, but patterns still shift.

Paul Morgan
June 2025

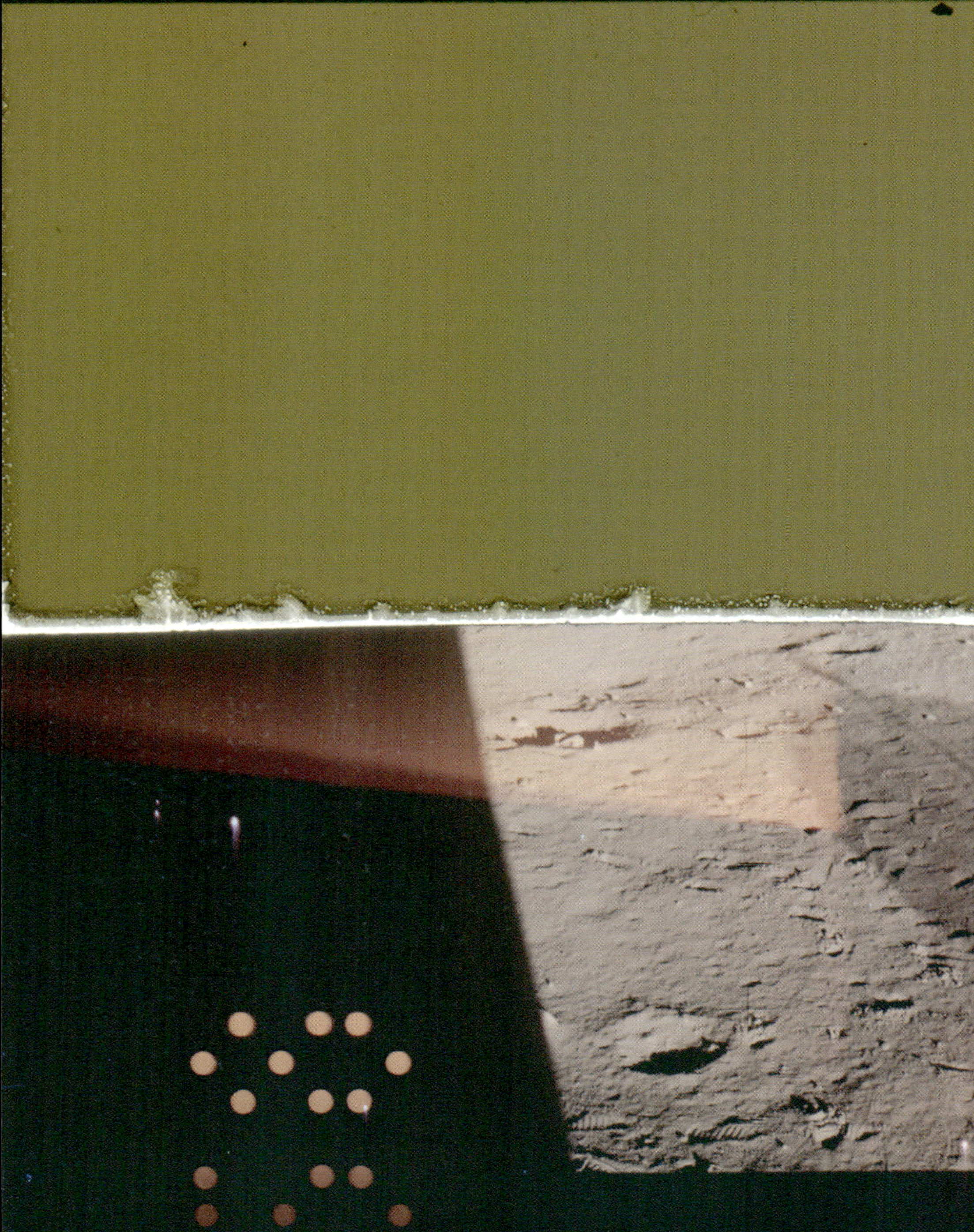

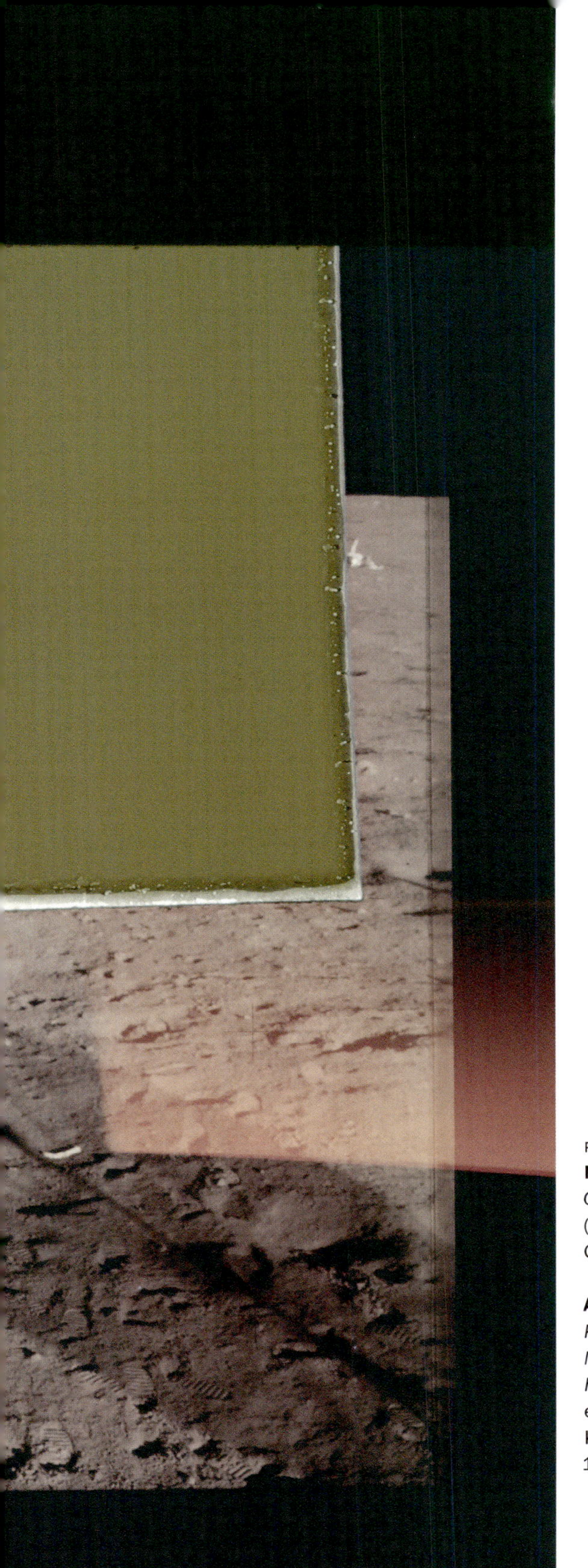

Mercury-Atlas 6, February 20, 1962
Overexposed Earth observation. Ansco Autoset (35mm); Fixed 50mm f/2.8 lens; Eastman Color Negative Film 5250.

Apollo 7, November 19, 1969
Partial view of lunar surface near the Lunar Module. Image taken during the first extravehicular activity. Hasselblad 500EL Data Camera (70mm); Zeiss Biogon 60mm f/5.6 lens; Kodak Ektachrome SO-168 EF High Speed ASA 160 Color Reversal Film.

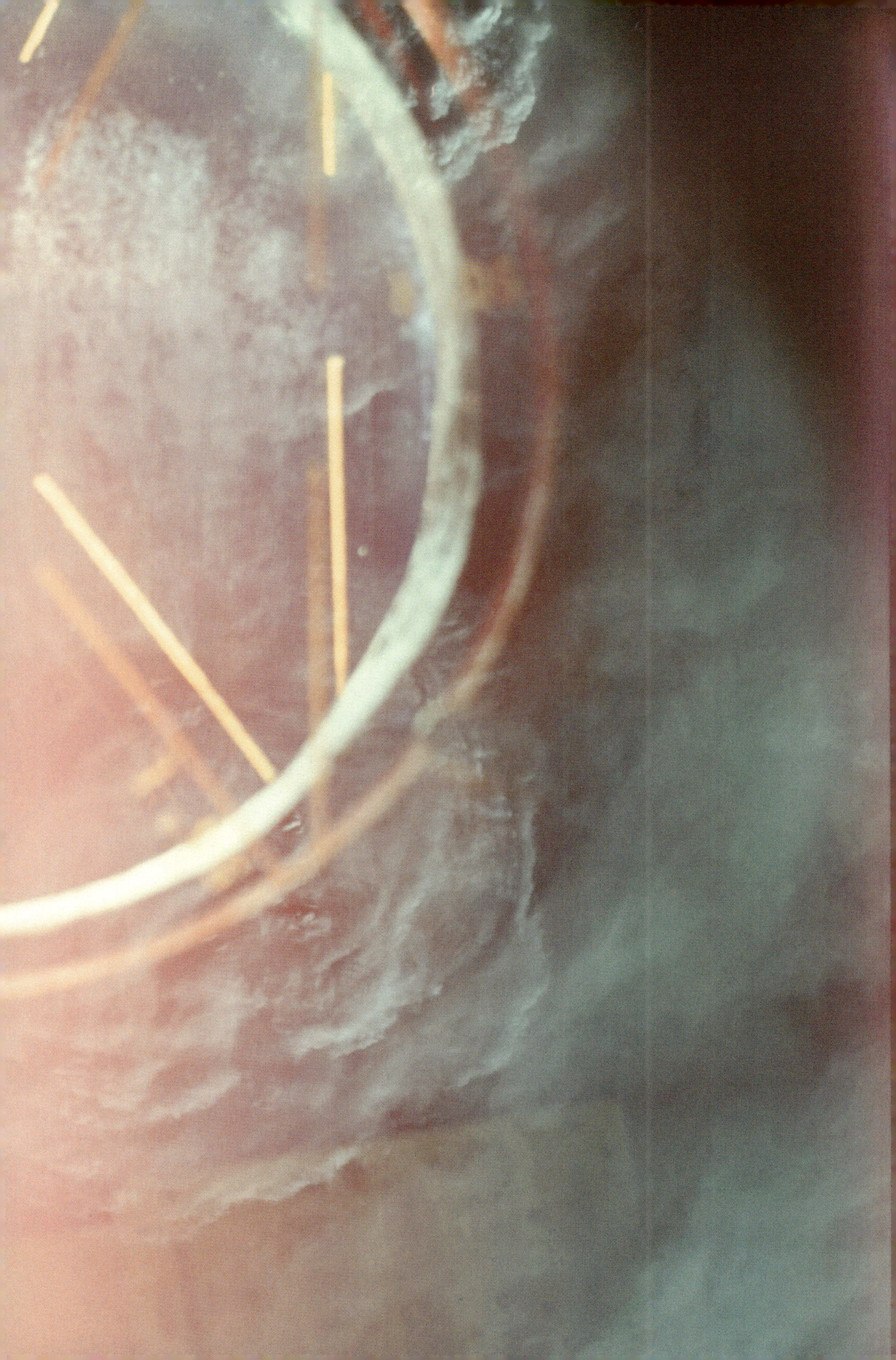

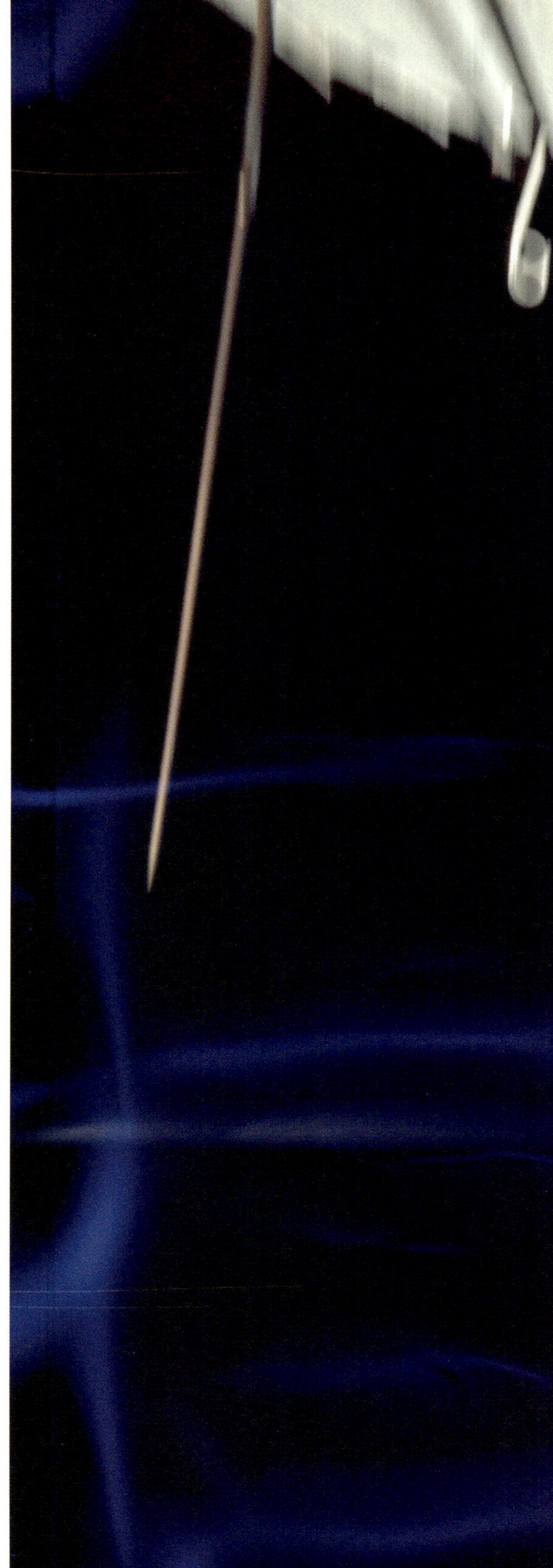

Apollo 7, October 11, 1968
*Cirrus, cumulonimbus clouds. Dark, near
vertical. Cloud cover: 100%.* Hasselblad 500C
(70mm); Zeiss Planar 80mm f/2.8 lens; Kodak
Ektachrome SO-368 Medium Speed ASA 64
Color Reversal Film.

Gemini 9, June 5, 1966
*Taken with Commander Eugene A. Cernan's
Extravehicular Activity camera during orbit
number 32.* Hasselblad Super-Wide Camera
(70mm); Zeiss Biogon 38mm f/4.5 lens; Kodak
Ektachrome SO-217 Medium Speed ASA 64
Color Reversal Film.

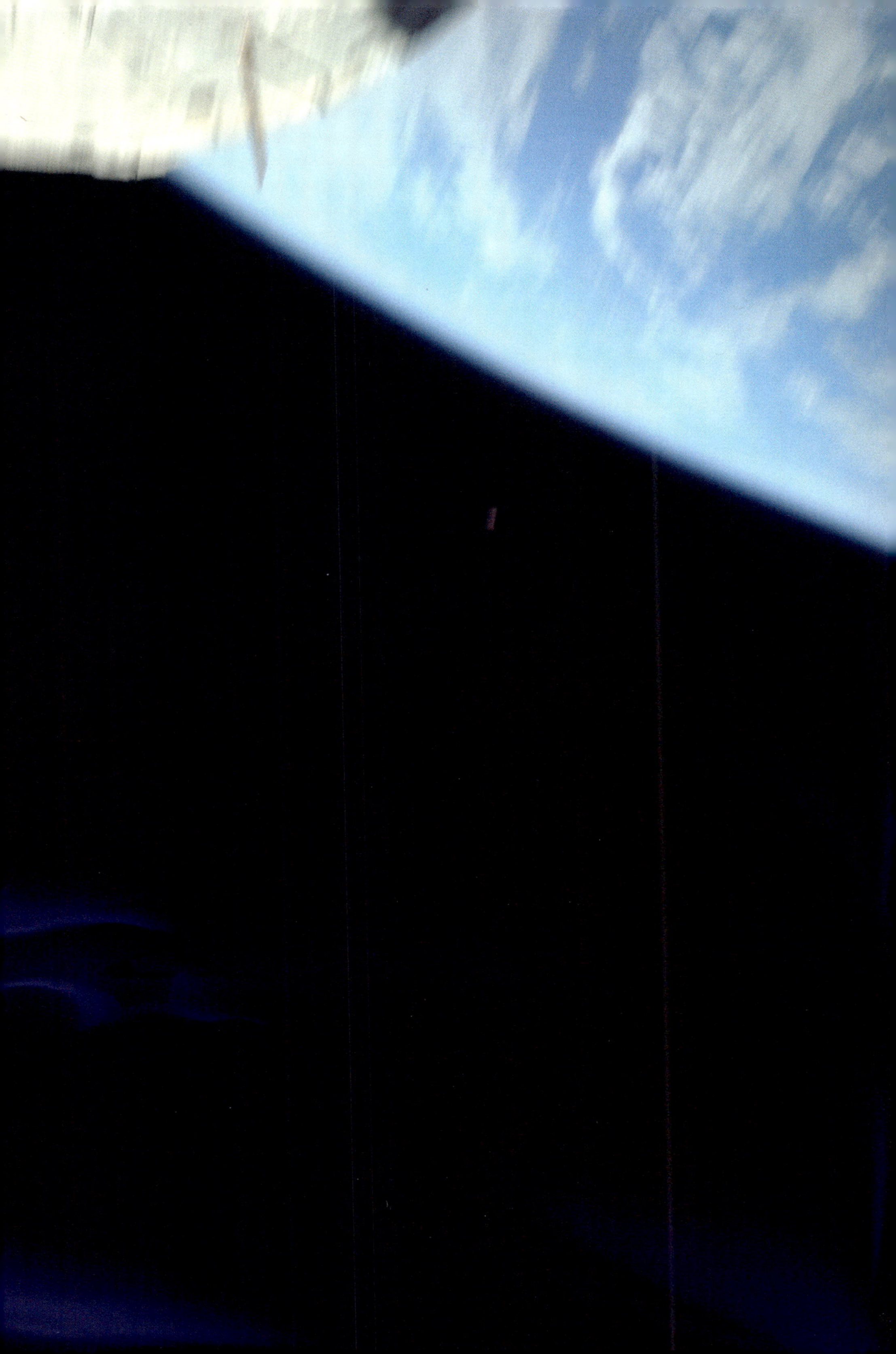

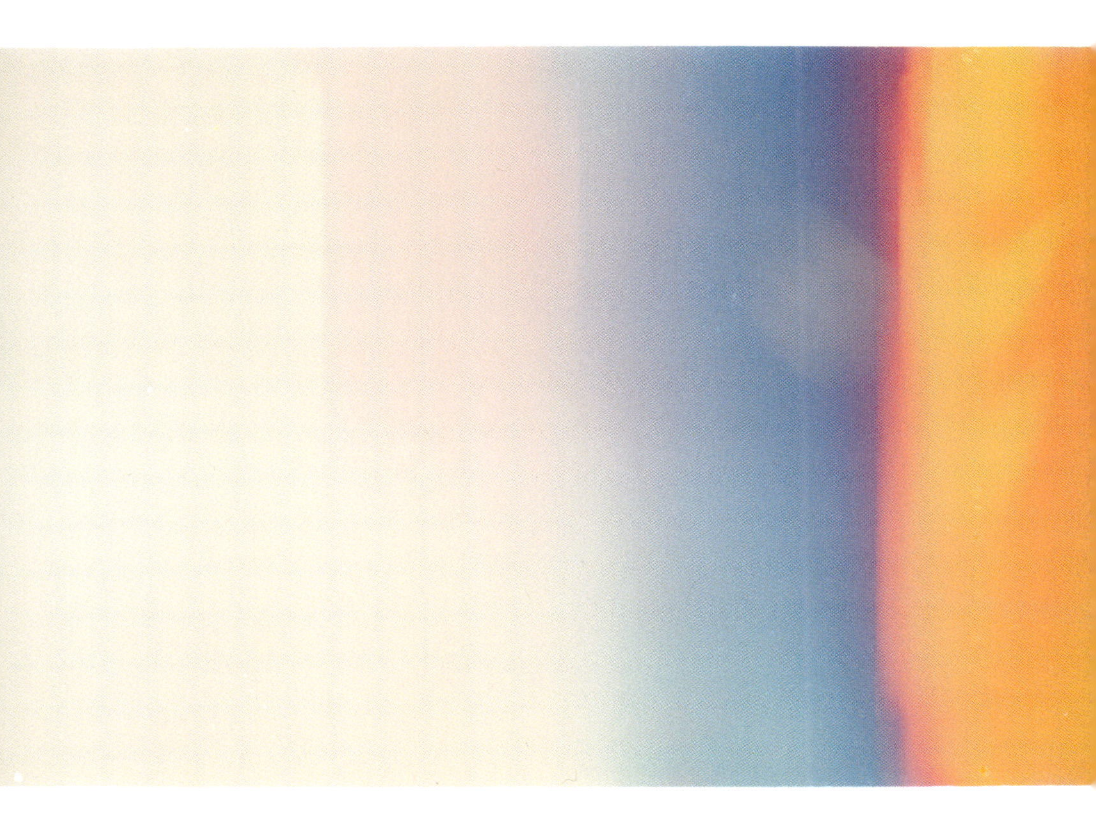

Mercury-Atlas 7, May 24, 1962
Overexposed Earth observation. Robot Recorder 36 (35mm); Schneider Xenar 45mm f/2.8
lens; Eastman Color Negative Film 5250.

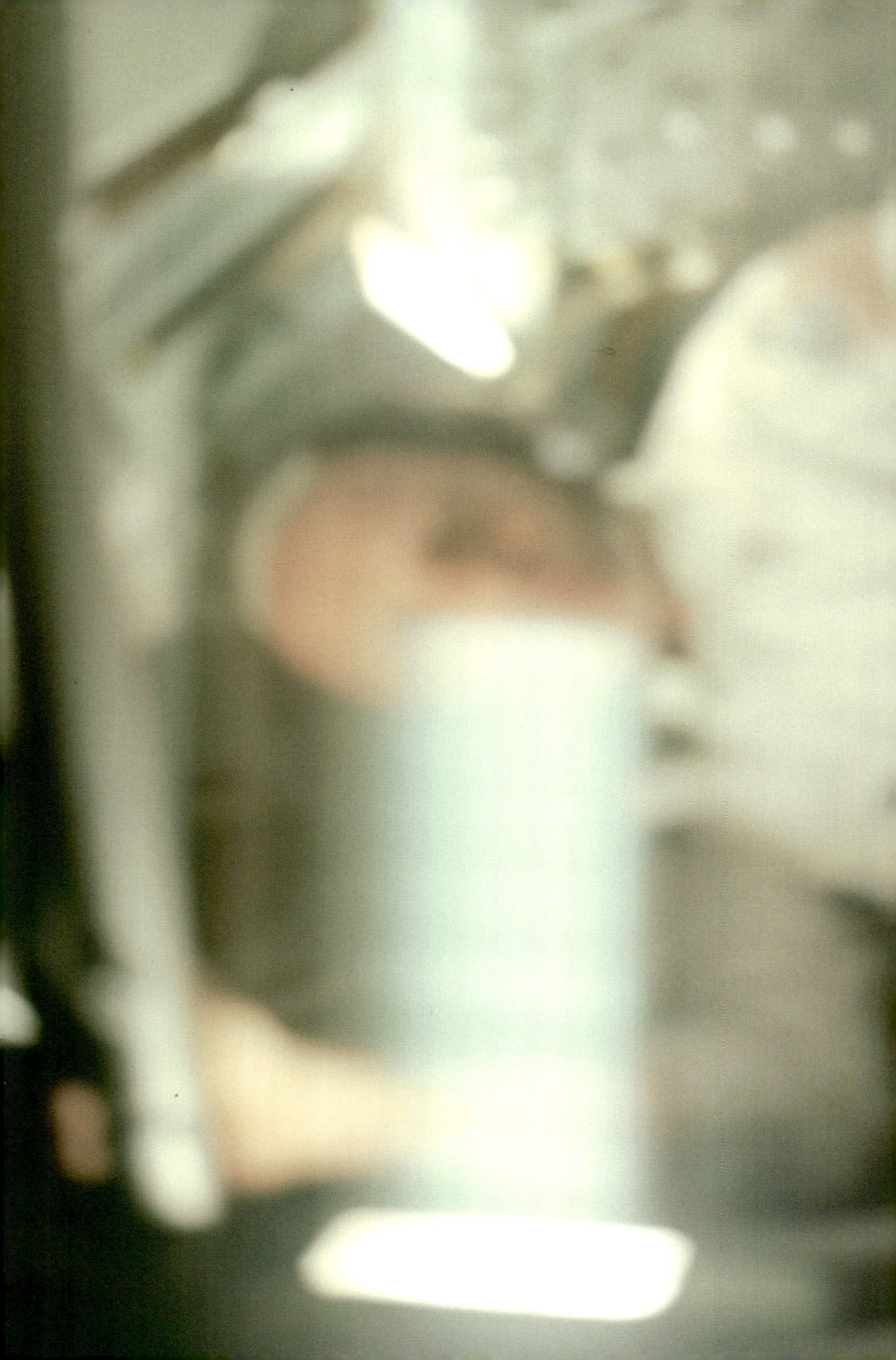

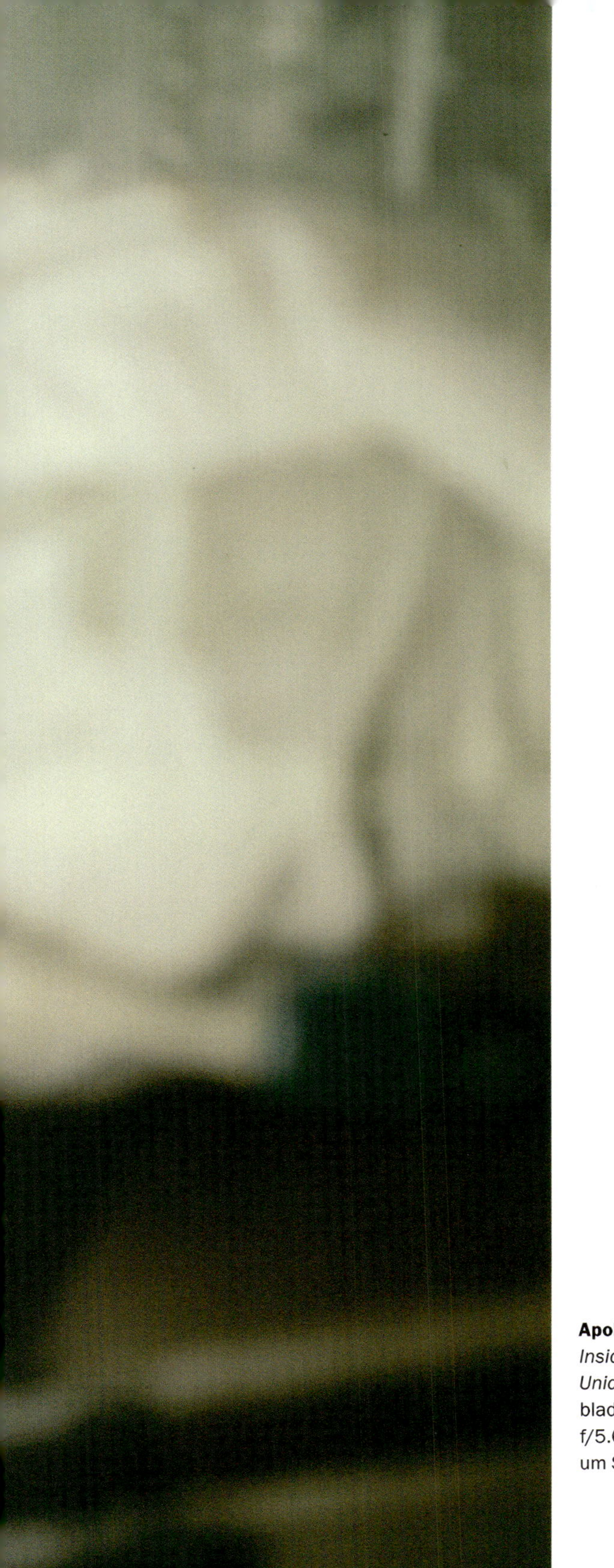

Apollo 10, May 18, 1969
Inside view of the Command Service Module.
Unidentified astronaut out of focus. Hasselblad 500EL (70mm); Zeiss Sonnar 250mm
f/5.6 lens; Kodak Ektachrome SO-368 Medium Speed ASA 64 Color Reversal Film.

Apollo 15, August 1, 1971
View of Station 7 and boulder taken during the second Extravehicular Activity. Hasselblad 500EL Data Camera (70mm); Zeiss Biogon 60mm f/5.6 lens; Kodak Ektachrome SO-168 EF High Speed ASA 160 Color Reversal Film.

Gemini 10, July 18, 1966
Clouds over water. Maurer Space Camera (70mm); Schneider Xenotar 80mm f/2.8 lens; Kodak Ektachrome SO-217 Medium Speed ASA 64 Color Reversal Film.

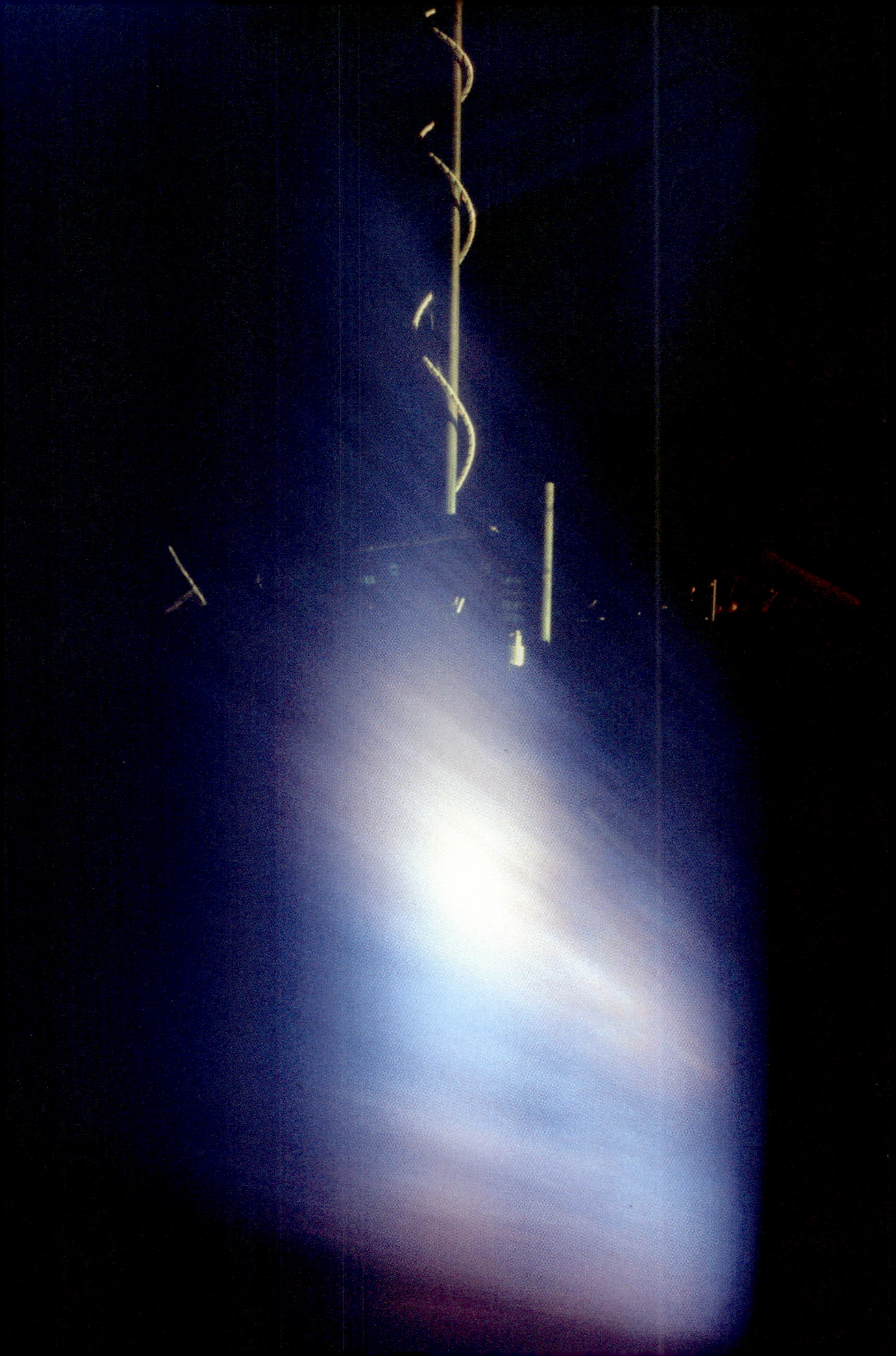

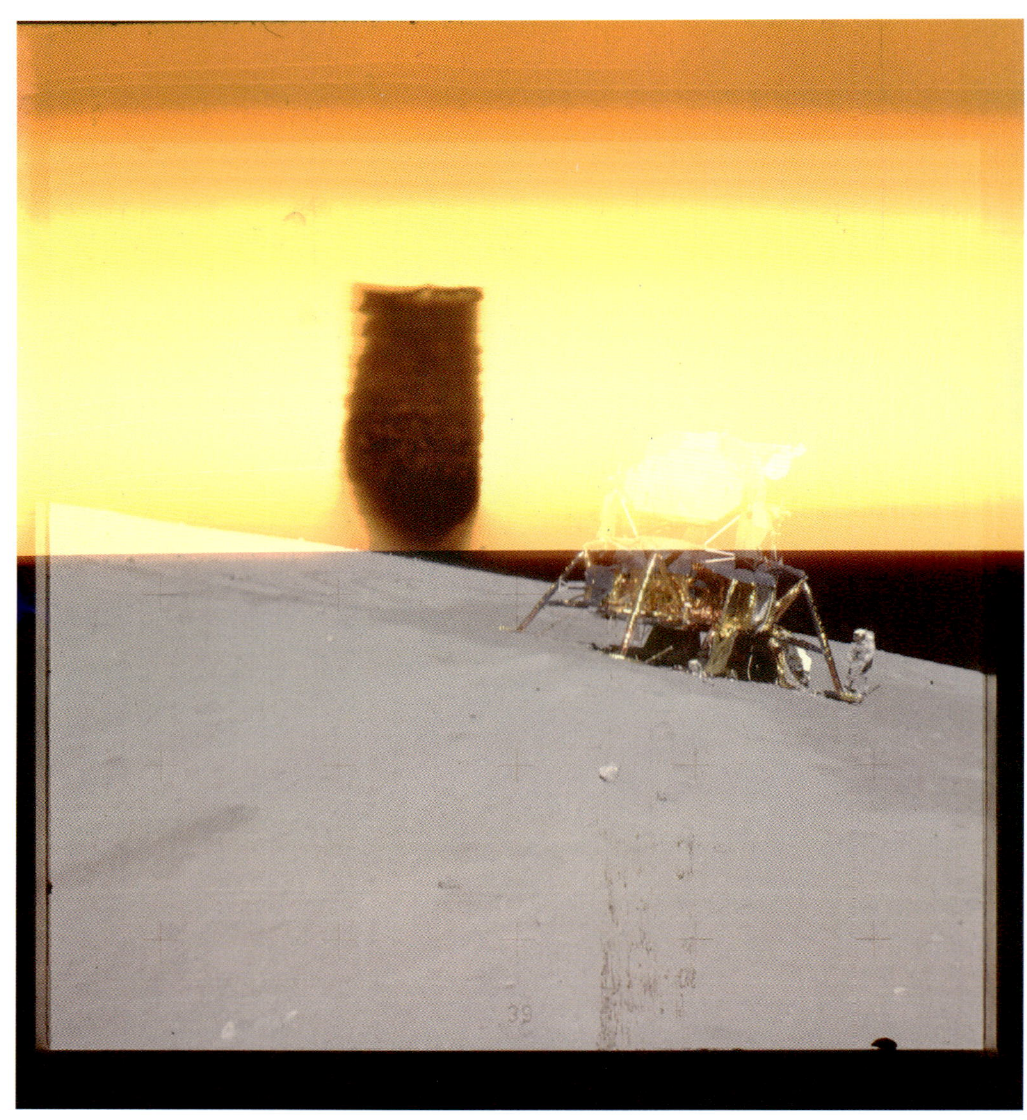

Apollo 16, April 25, 1972
*View of Station East of Lunar Module and
Lunar Moduel Pilot taken during the third
Extravehicular Activity.* Hasselblad 500EL
Data Camera (70mm); Zeiss Biogon 60mm
f/5.6 lens; Kodak Ektachrome SO-168 EF High
Speed ASA 160 Color Reversal Film.

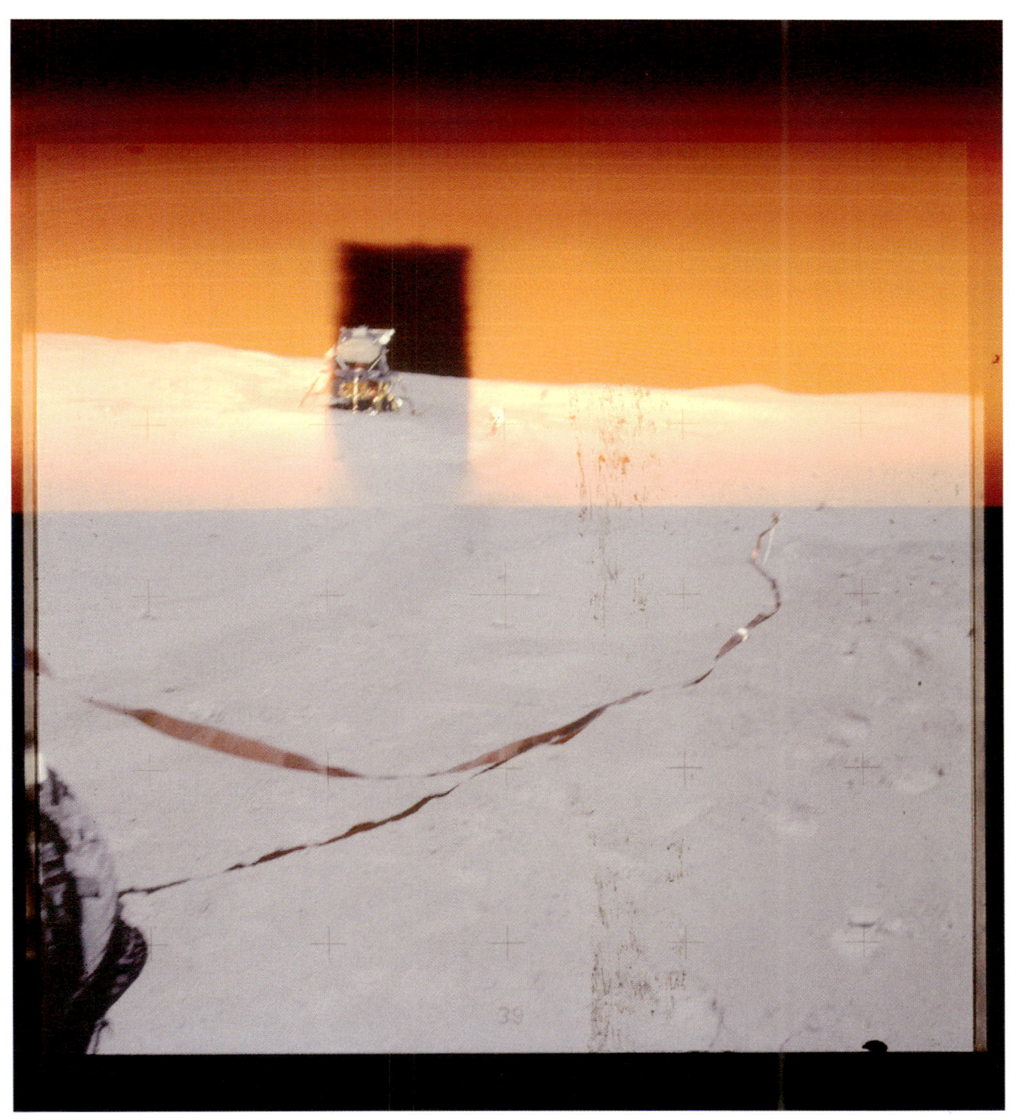

Apollo 16, April 25, 1972

View of Station East of Lunar Module, Magne-tometer, and Lunar Module taken during the third Extravehicular Activity. Hasselblad 500EL Data Camera (70mm); Zeiss Biogon 60mm f/5.6 lens; Kodak Ektachrome SO-168 EF High Speed ASA 160 Color Reversal Film.

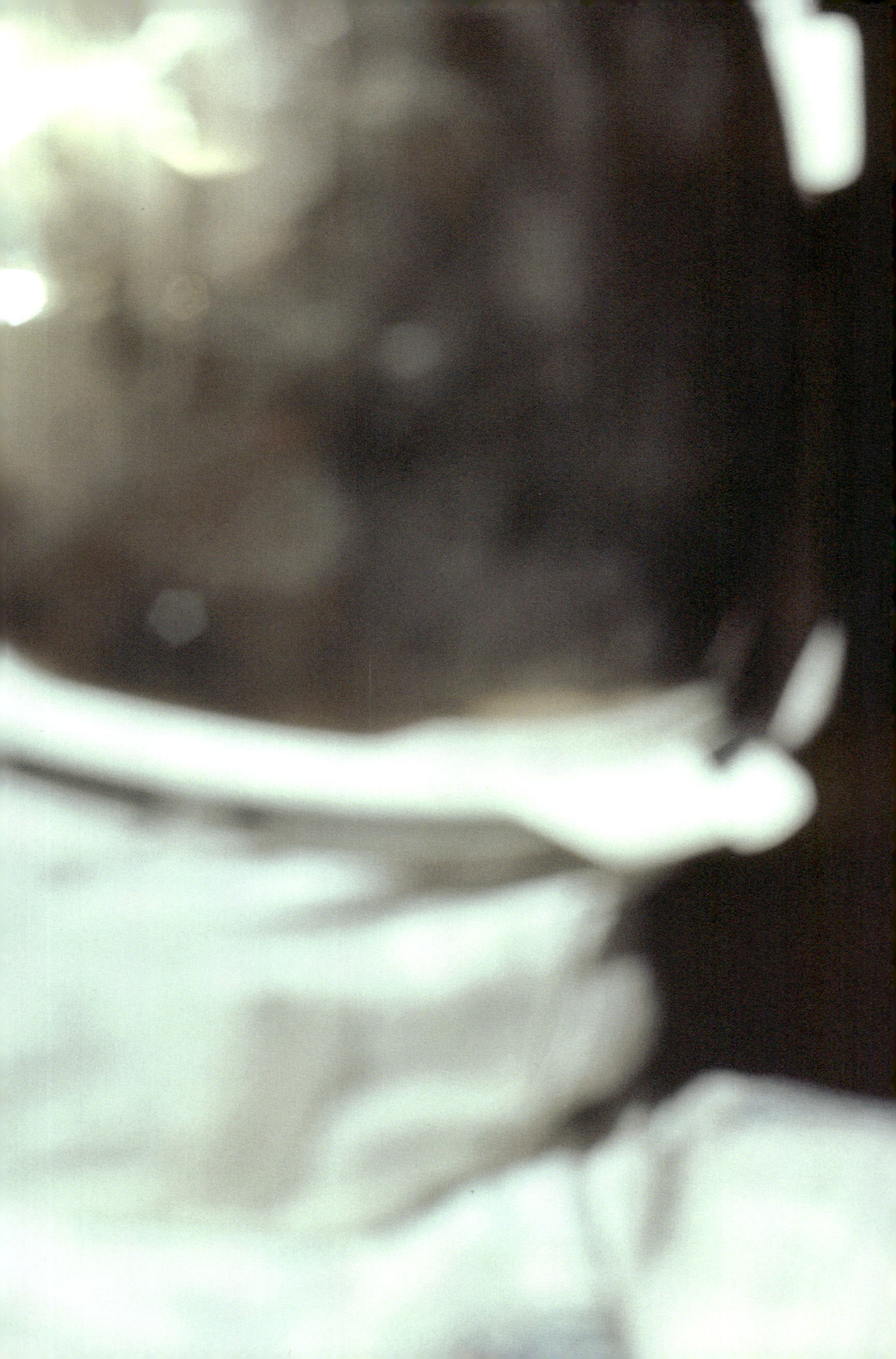

Apollo 17, December 17, 1972
Unfocused view of astronaut Ronald Ev-
ans, Command Service Module Pilot, as he
performs an Extravehicular Activity, retrieving
film from cameras stowed in the Scientific
Instrument Module Bay of the CSM. Image
taken on Trans-Earth Coast. Hasselblad 500EL
(70mm); Zeiss Planar 80mm f/2.8 lens; Kodak
Ektachrome SO-368 Medium Speed ASA 64
Color Reversal Film.

Mercury-Atlas 6, February 20, 1962
Unclear. Ansco Autoset (35mm); Fixed 50mm
f/2.8 lens; Eastman Color Negative Film 5250.

*Double exposure of the Gemini 7 spacecraft—
side view—taken from the Gemini 6 spacecraft during rendezvous and station keeping
maneuvers at an altitude of 157 nautical
miles during orbit number 7.* Hasselblad 500C
(70mm); Zeiss Planar 80mm f/2.8 lens; Kodak
Ektachrome SO-217 Medium Speed ASA 64
Color Reversal Film.

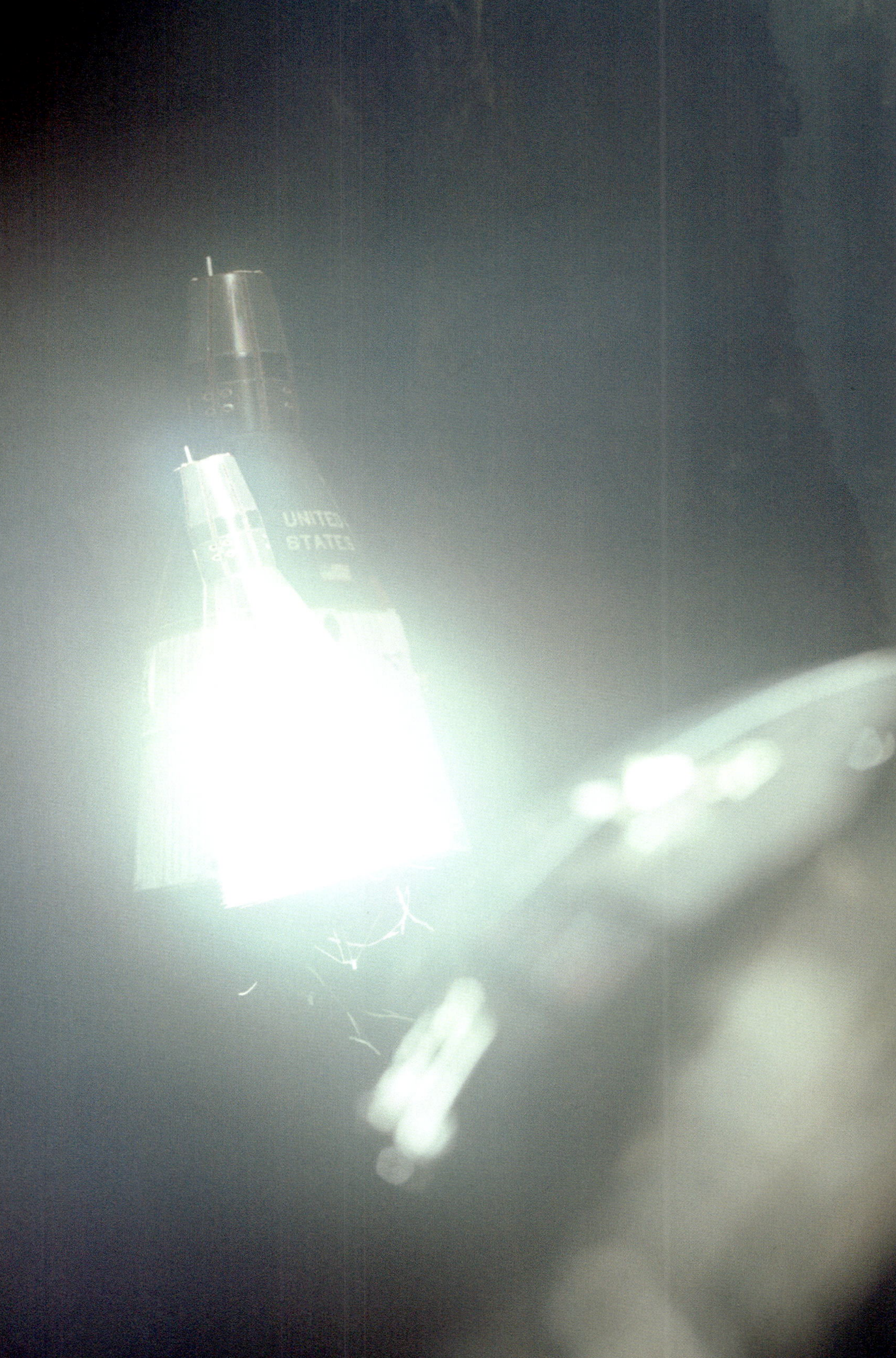

UNITED
STATES

Mercury-Atlas 7, May 24, 1962

Overexposed Earth observation. Robot Recorder 36 (35mm); Schneider Xenar 45mm f/2.8 lens; Eastman Color Negative Film 5250.

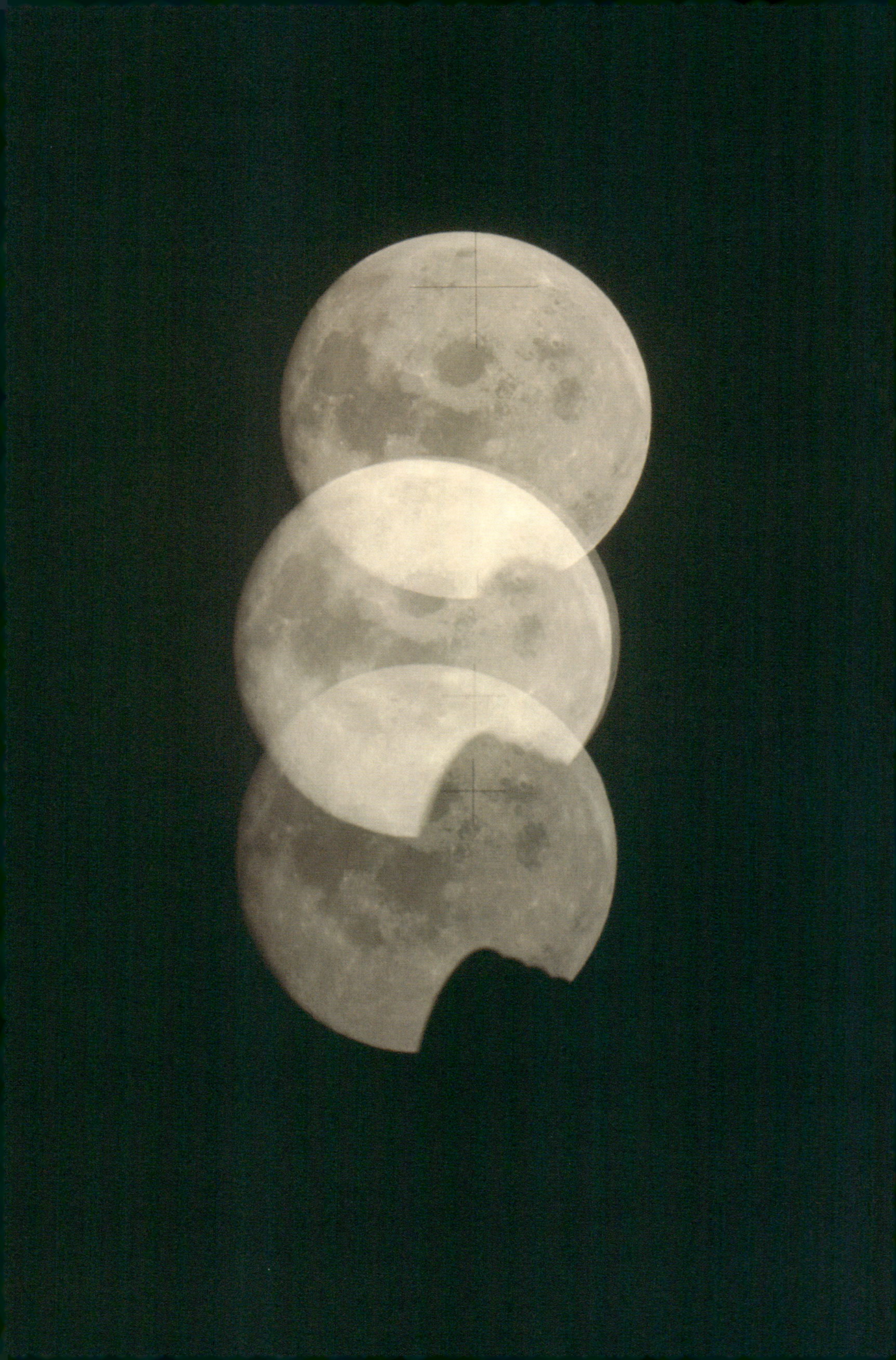

Apollo 13, April 14, 1970
Triple exposure view of the lunar surface seen as the spacecraft recedes from the Moon back towards the Earth. Hasselblad 500EL (70mm); Zeiss Sonnar 250mm f/5.6 lens; Kodak Ektachrome SO-168 EF High Speed ASA 160 Color Reversal Film.

Mercury-Atlas 6, February 20, 1962
Overexposed Earth observation. Ansco Autoset
(35mm); Fixed 50mm f/2.8 lens; Eastman
Color Negative Film 5250.

Gemini 6, December 15, 1965
*Gemini 7 spacecraft—adapter end, partial
frame—taken from the Gemini 6 spacecraft
during rendezvous and station keeping
maneuvers at an altitude of 166 nautical
miles during orbit number 6.* Hasselblad 500C
(70mm); Zeiss Planar 80mm f/2.8 lens; Kodak
Ektachrome SO-217 Medium Speed ASA 64
Color Reversal Film.

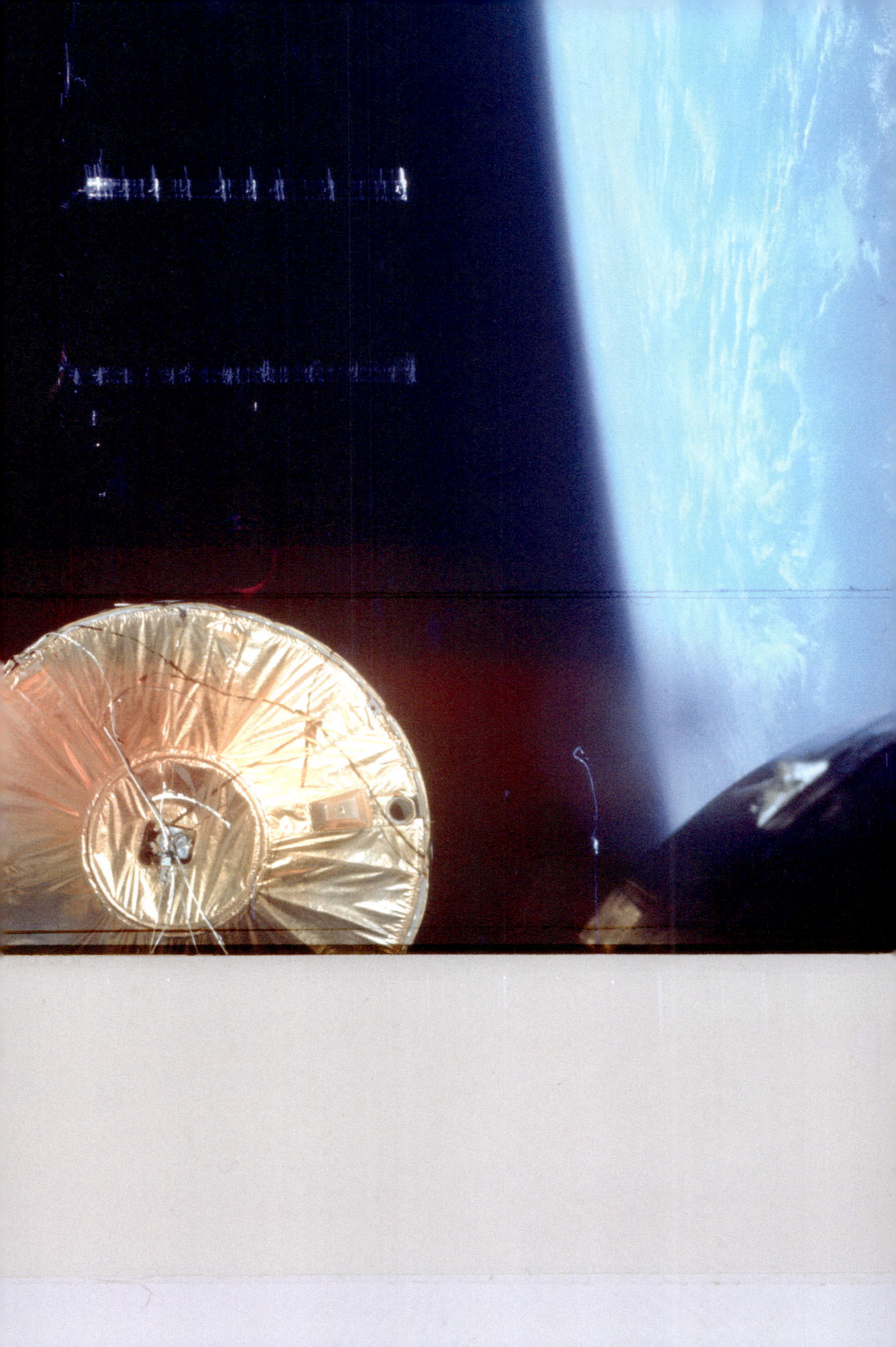

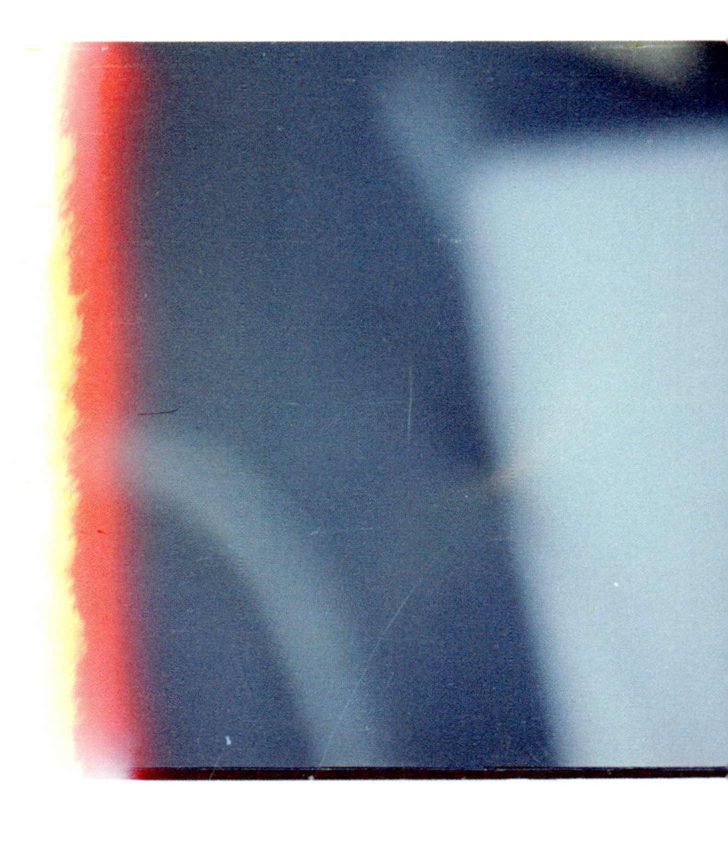

Mercury-Atlas 6, February 20, 1962
Overexposed Earth observation. Ansco Autoset (35mm); Fixed 50mm f/2.8 lens; Eastman Color Negative Film 5250.

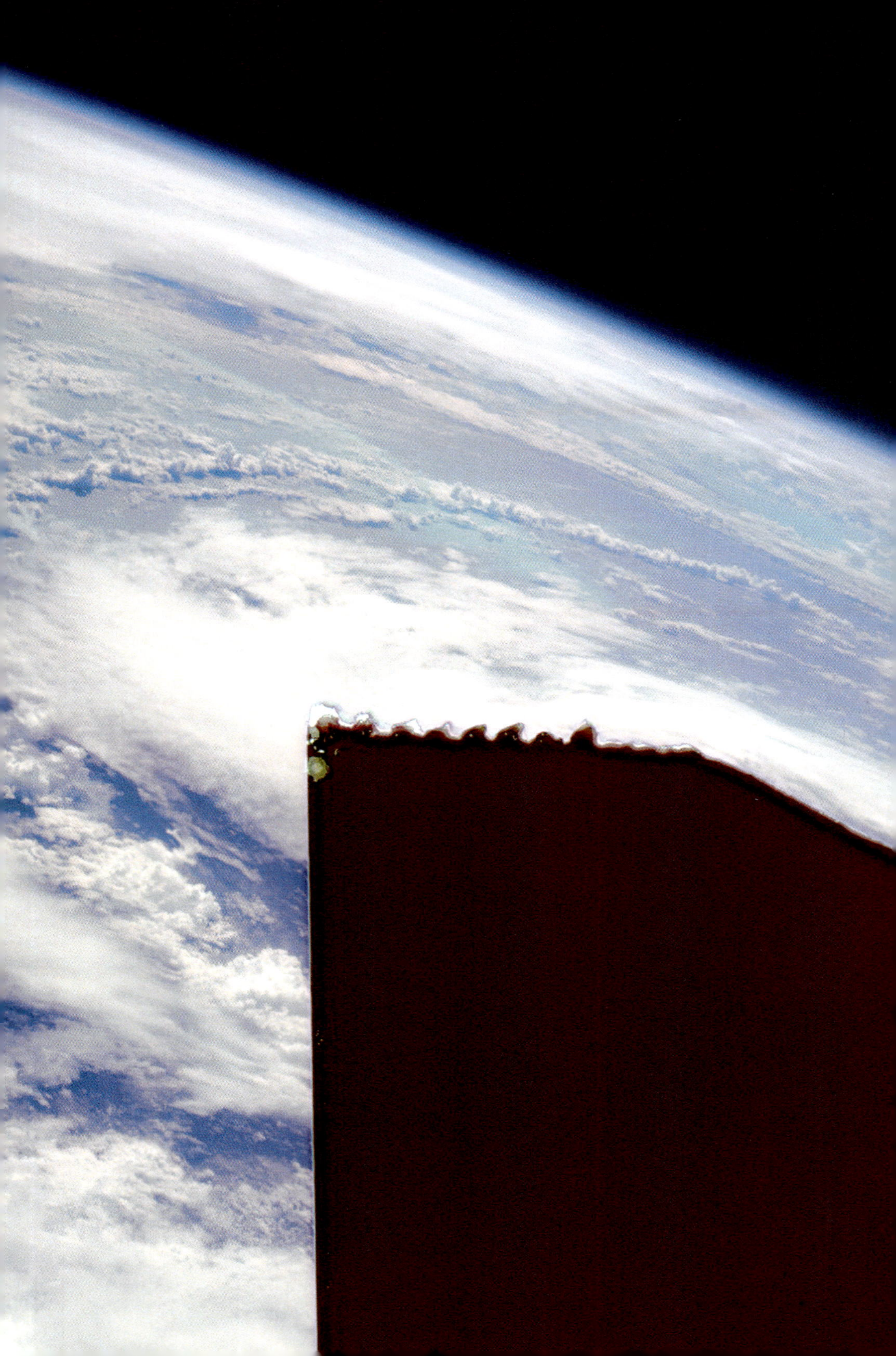

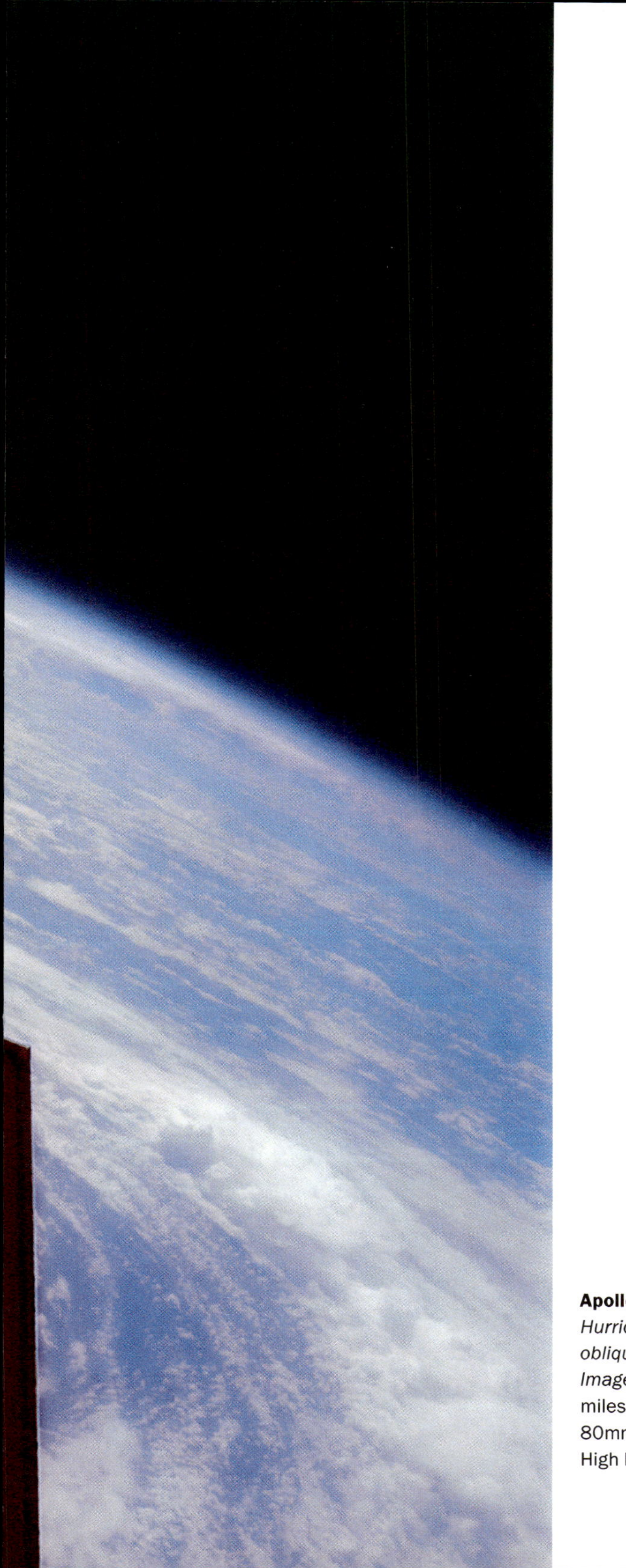

Apollo 7, October 11, 1968

Hurricane Gladys in the Gulf of Mexico. High oblique. Earth Limb visible. Cloud Cover 99%. Image taken on revolution 91. Altitude: 99 miles. Hasselblad 500C (70mm); Zeiss Planar 80mm f/2.8 lens; Kodak Ektachrome SO-121 High Resolution Aerial Color Film.

Apollo 16, April 24, 1972
*Blank image taken between the first and sec-
ond Extravehicular Activity.* Hasselblad 500EL
Data Camera (70mm); Zeiss Biogon 60mm
f/5.6 lens; Kodak Ektachrome SO-168 EF High
Speed ASA 160 Color Reversal Film.

Apollo 10, May 24, 1969
Hasselblad 500EL (70mm); 70mm lens; Kodak
Ektachrome SO-368 medium speed ASA 64
Color Reversal Film.

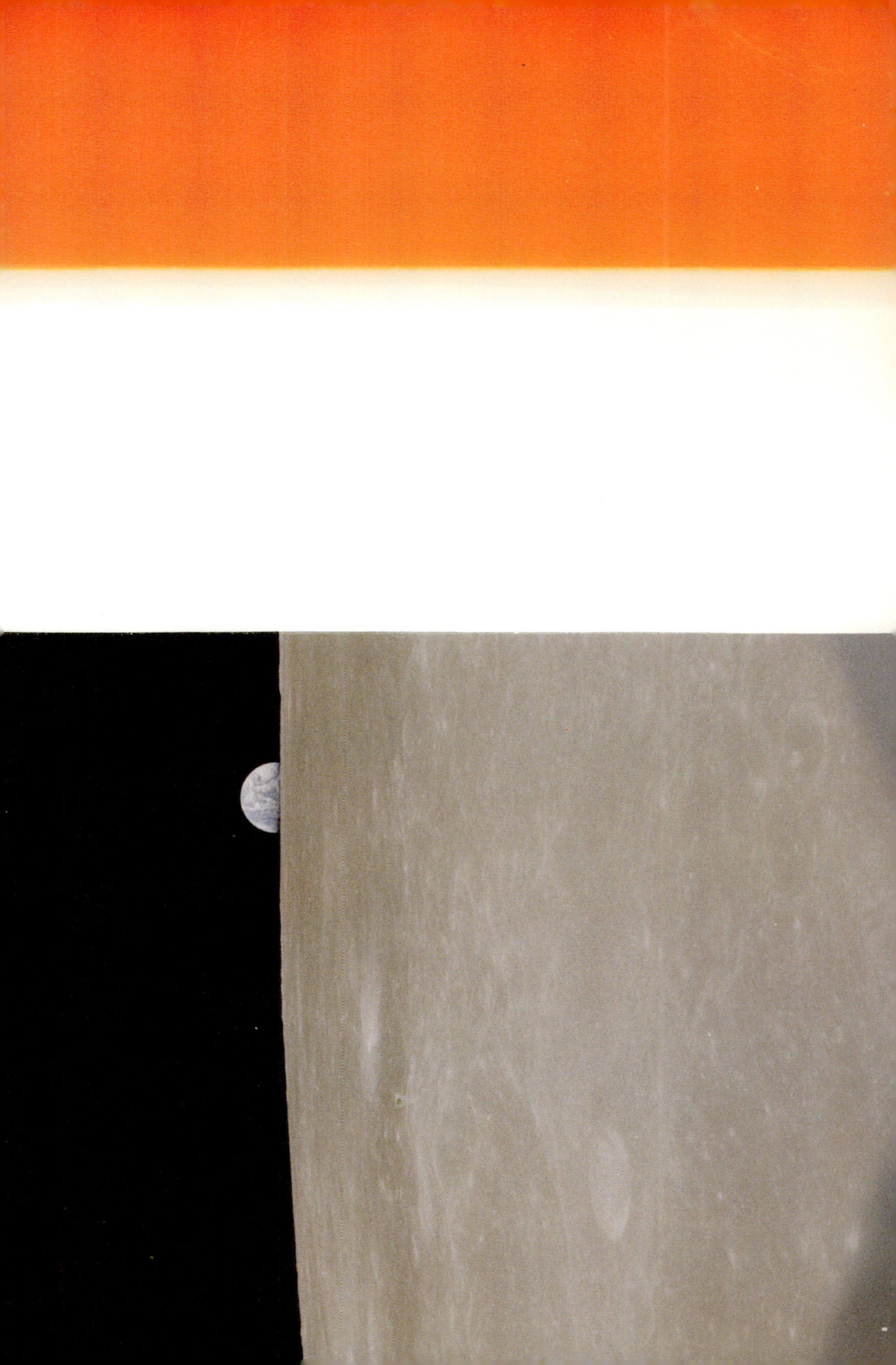

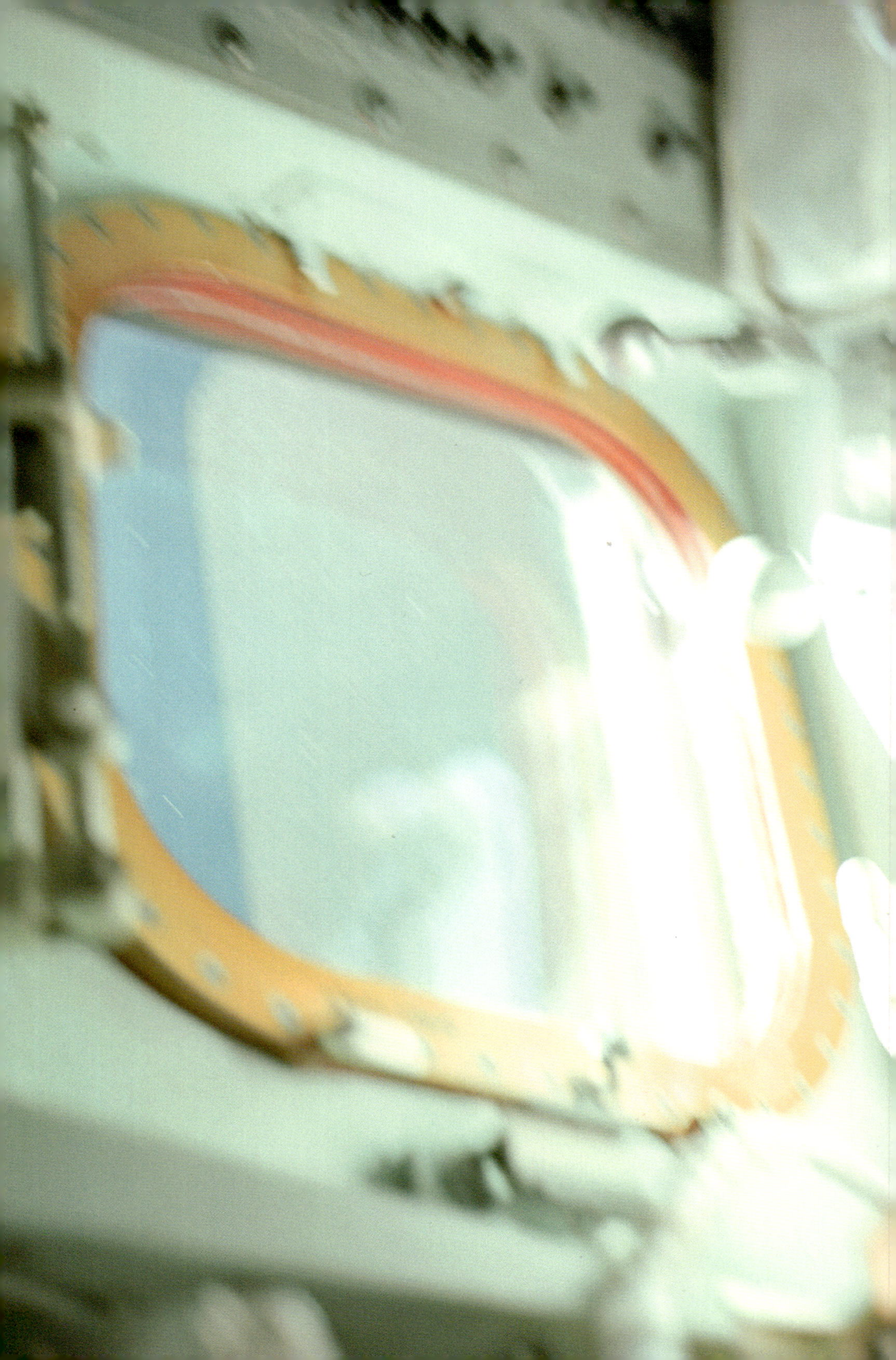

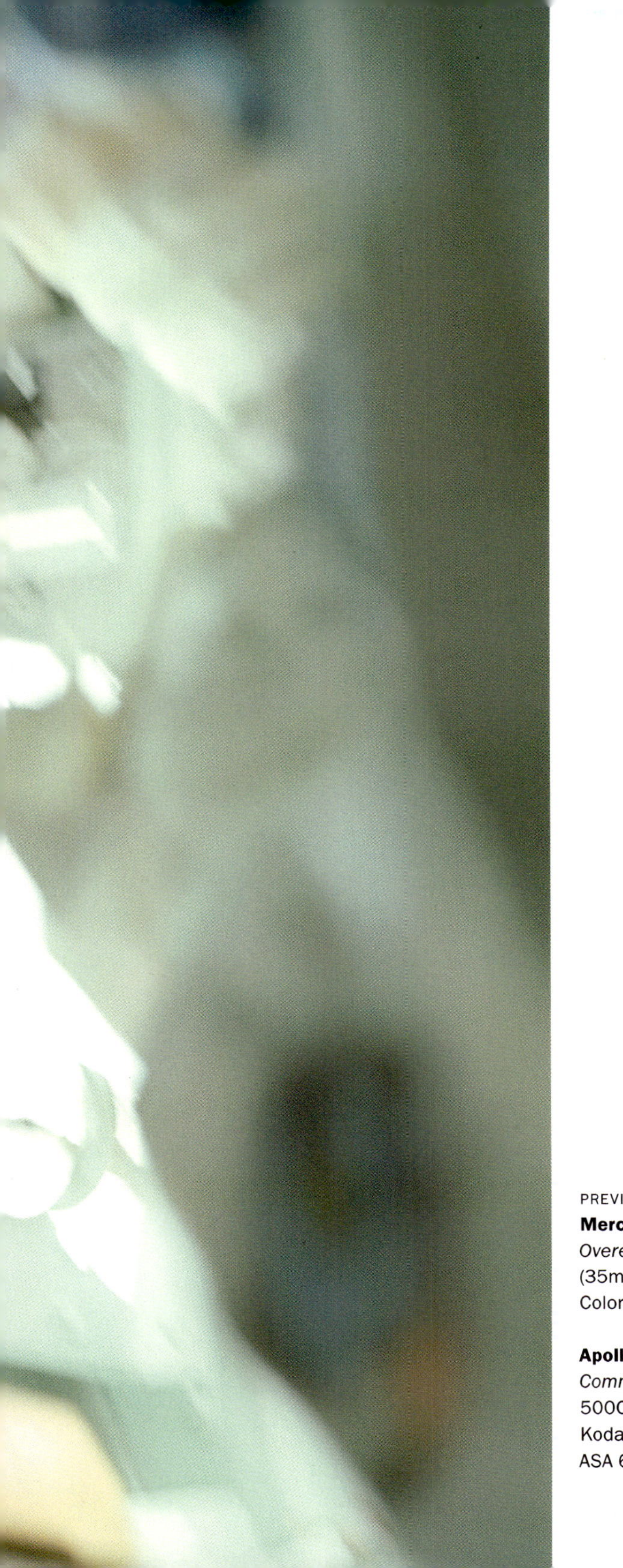

Mercury-Atlas 6, February 20, 1962
Overexposed Earth observation. Ansco Autoset
(35mm); Fixed 50mm f/2.8 lens; Eastman
Color Negative Film 5250.

Apollo 7, October 11, 1968
Command Module window, glare. Hasselblad
500C (70mm); Zeiss Planar 80mm f/2.8 lens;
Kodak Ektachrome SO-368 Medium Speed
ASA 64 Color Reversal Film.

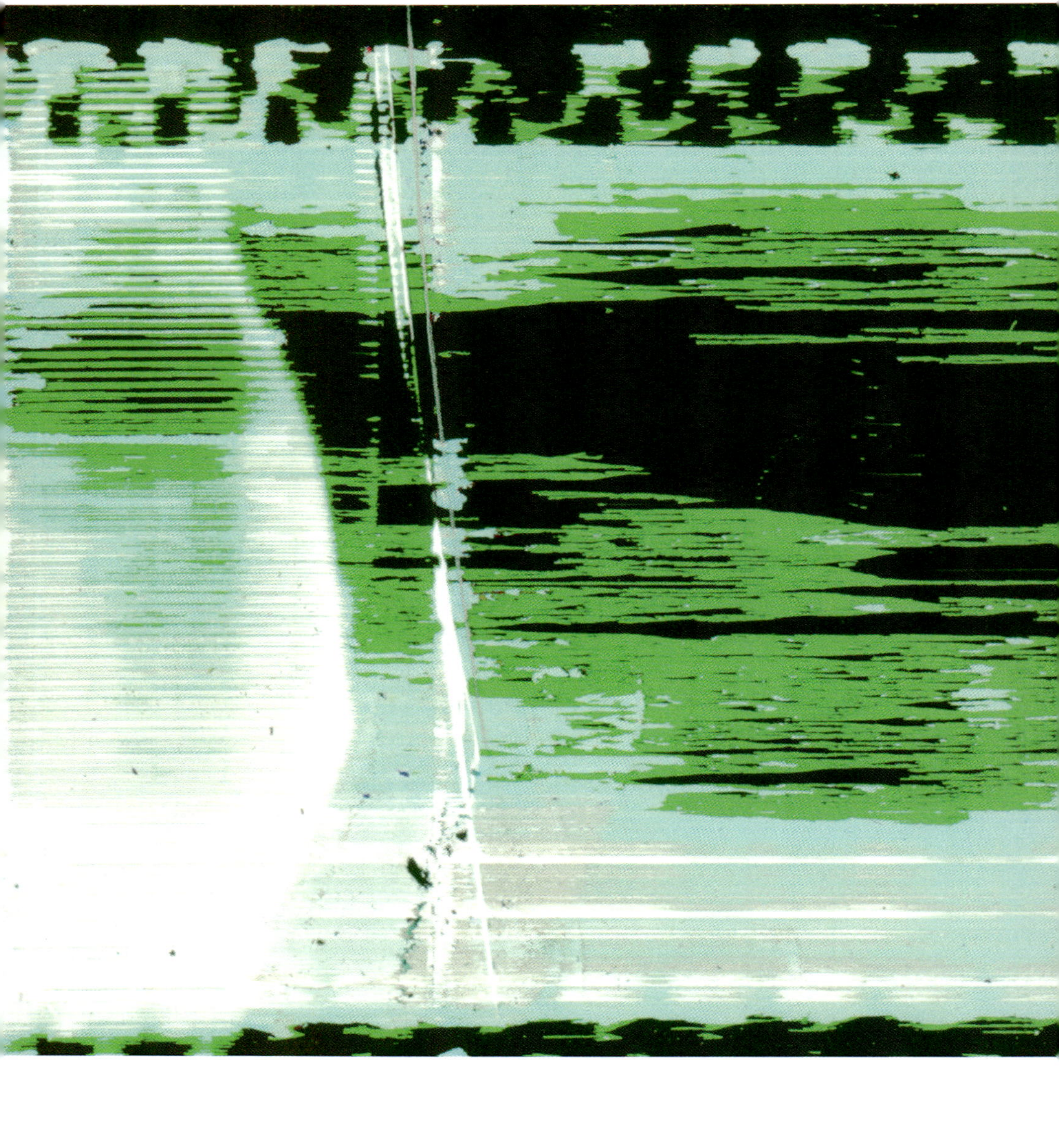

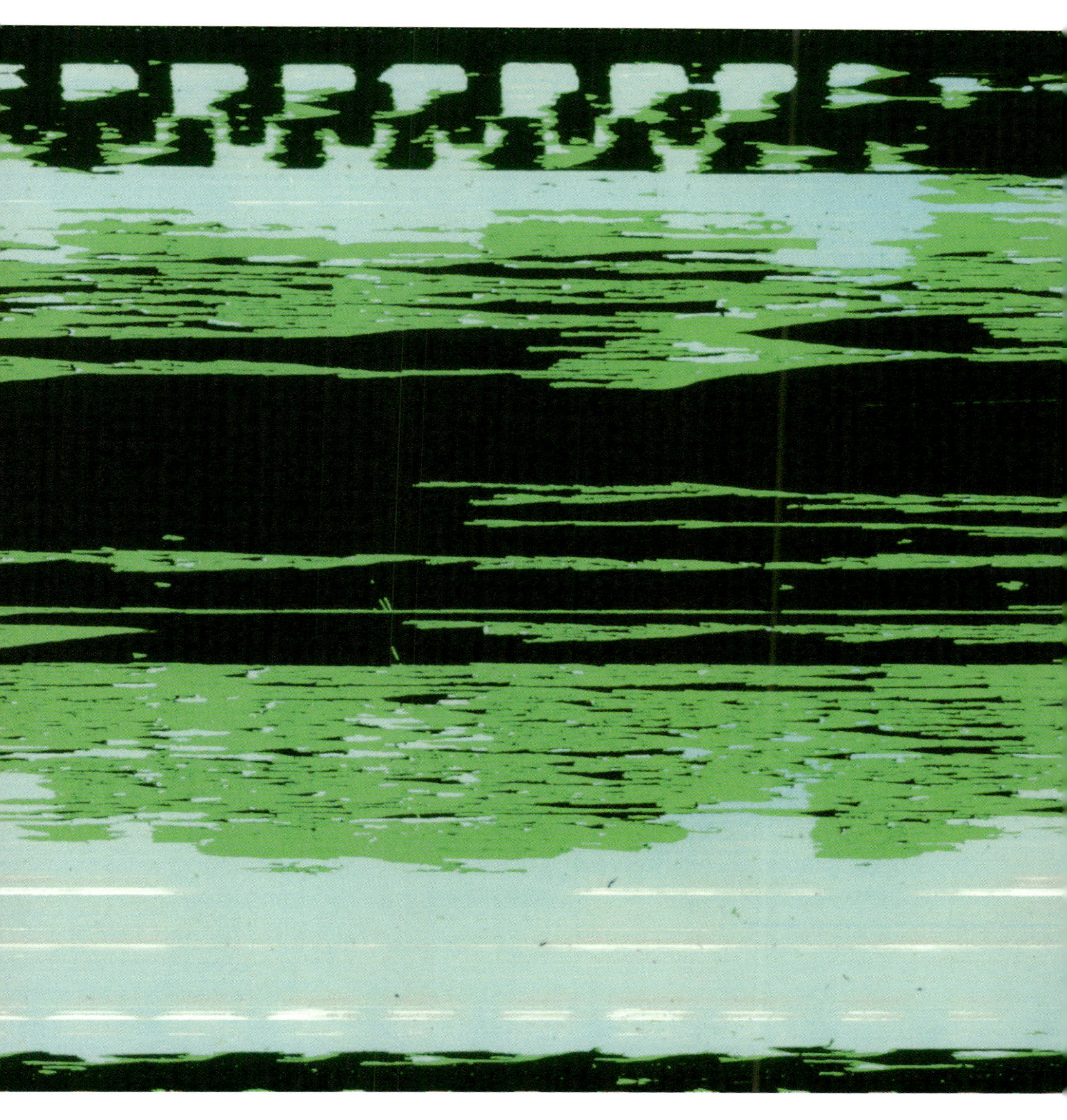

Apollo 6, April 4, 1968
Views of Earth. J. A. Maurer 220G (70mm);
Kodak Ektar 76mm f/2.8 lens; Kodak Ekta-
chrome SO-121 High Resolution Aerial ASA 64
Color Film.

Gemini 7, December 17, 1965
*Clouds over the Atlantic taken during orbit
number 195.* Hasselblad 500C (70mm);
Zeiss Planar 80mm f/2.8 lens; Kodak Ekta-
chrome SO-217 Medium Speed ASA 64 Color
Reversal Film.

Mercury-Atlas 6, February 20, 1962
Unclear. Ansco Autoset (35mm); Fixed 50mm
f/2.8 lens; Eastman Color Negative Film 5250.

Apollo 15, August 2, 1971
*The Apollo 15 subsatellite. Before transearth
injection the Command Service Module
launched a subsatellite containing three
experiments: the 8-band transponder, the
particle shadow/boundary layer experiment
and a magnetometer. Still photographs such
as these were used to document the condition
of the subsatellite surfaces and deployment of
the booms. The DAC photographers recorded
the spin rate and wobble of the spinning subsatellite. Image was taken during revolution
74.* Hasselblad 500EL (70mm); Zeiss Sonnar
250mm f/5.6 lens; Kodak Ektachrome SO-368
Medium Speed ASA 64 Color Reversal Film.

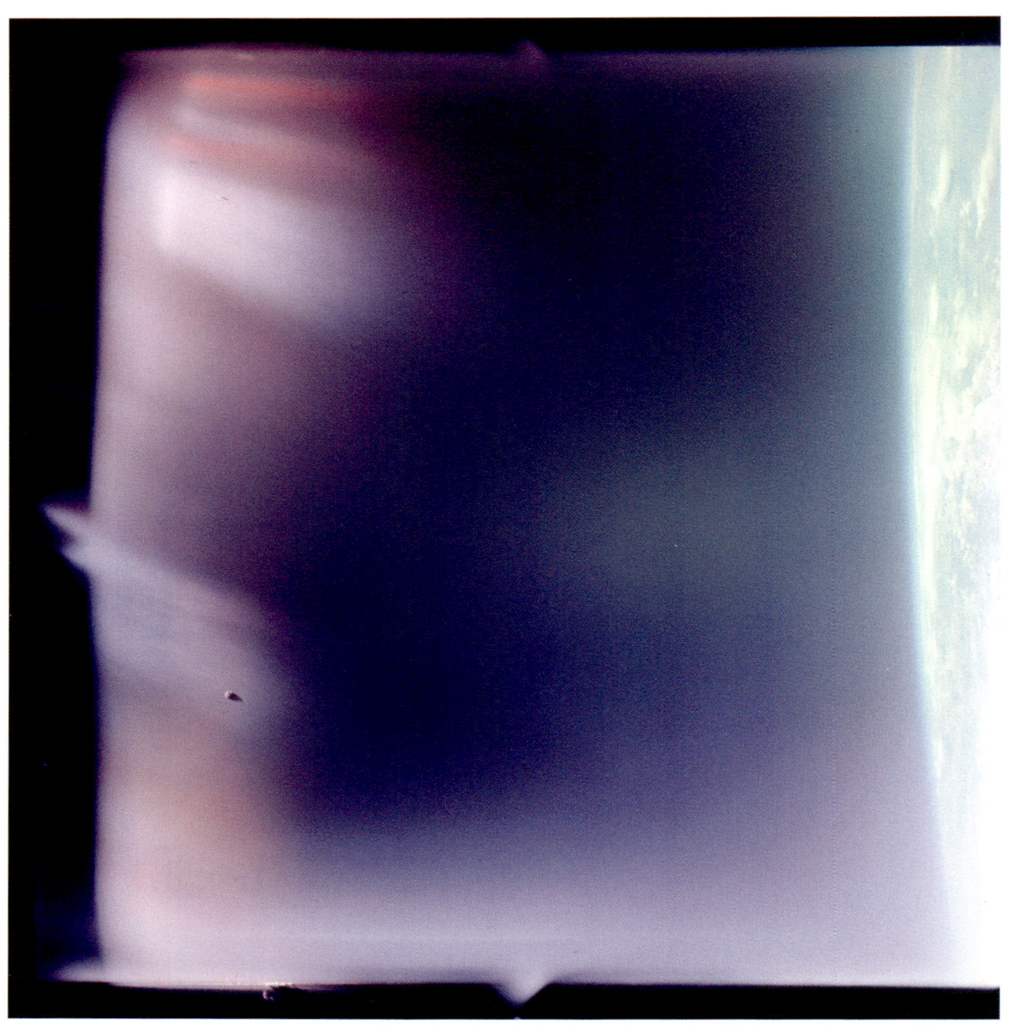

Gemini 10, July 18, 1966
*Clouds over China and North Vietnam taken
during orbit number 34.* Maurer Space Camera
(70mm); Schneider Xenotar 80mm f/2.8 lens;
Kodak Ektachrome SO-217 Medium Speed
ASA 64 Color Reversal Film.

Gemini 7, December 9, 1965

Overexposed. Hasselblad 500C (70mm); Zeiss Planar 80mm f/2.8 lens; Kodak Ektachrome 8443 Infrared Aerial Color Film.

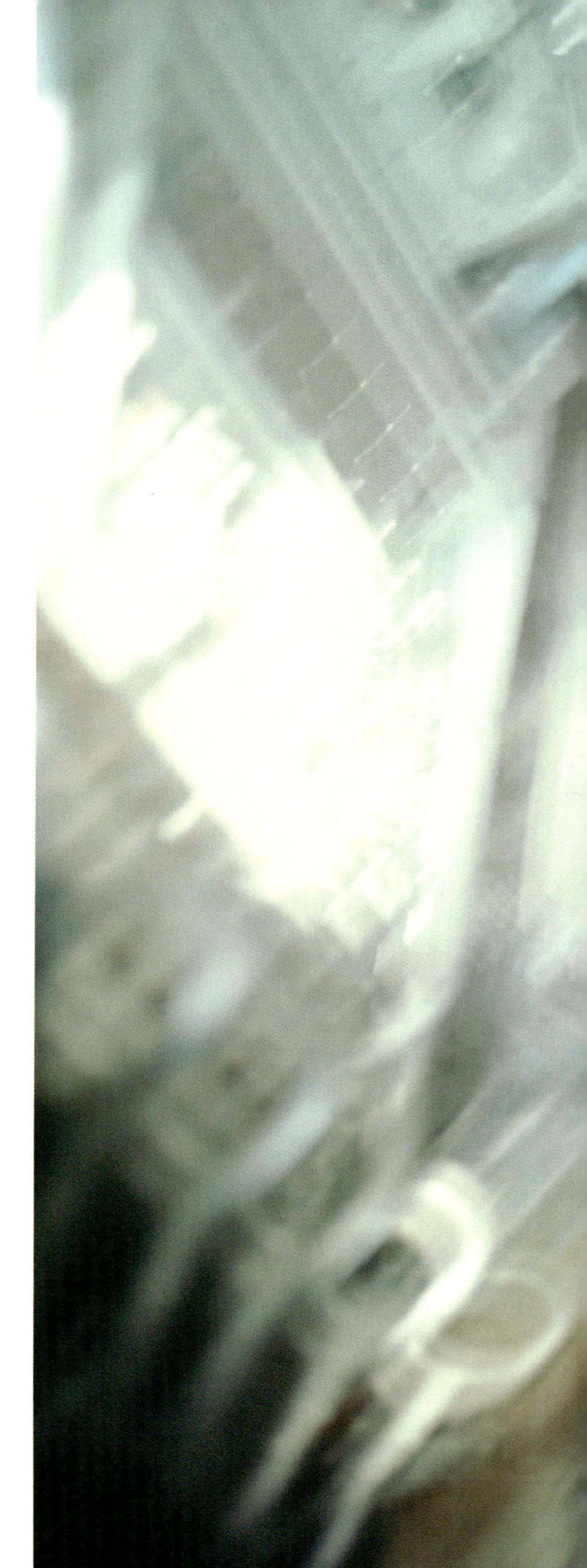

Gemini 5, August 25, 1965
Inside spacecraft taken during orbit number
65. Hasselblad 500C (70mm); Zeiss Planar
80mm f/2.8 lens; GAF Super Anscochrome
D-50 Color Reversal Film.

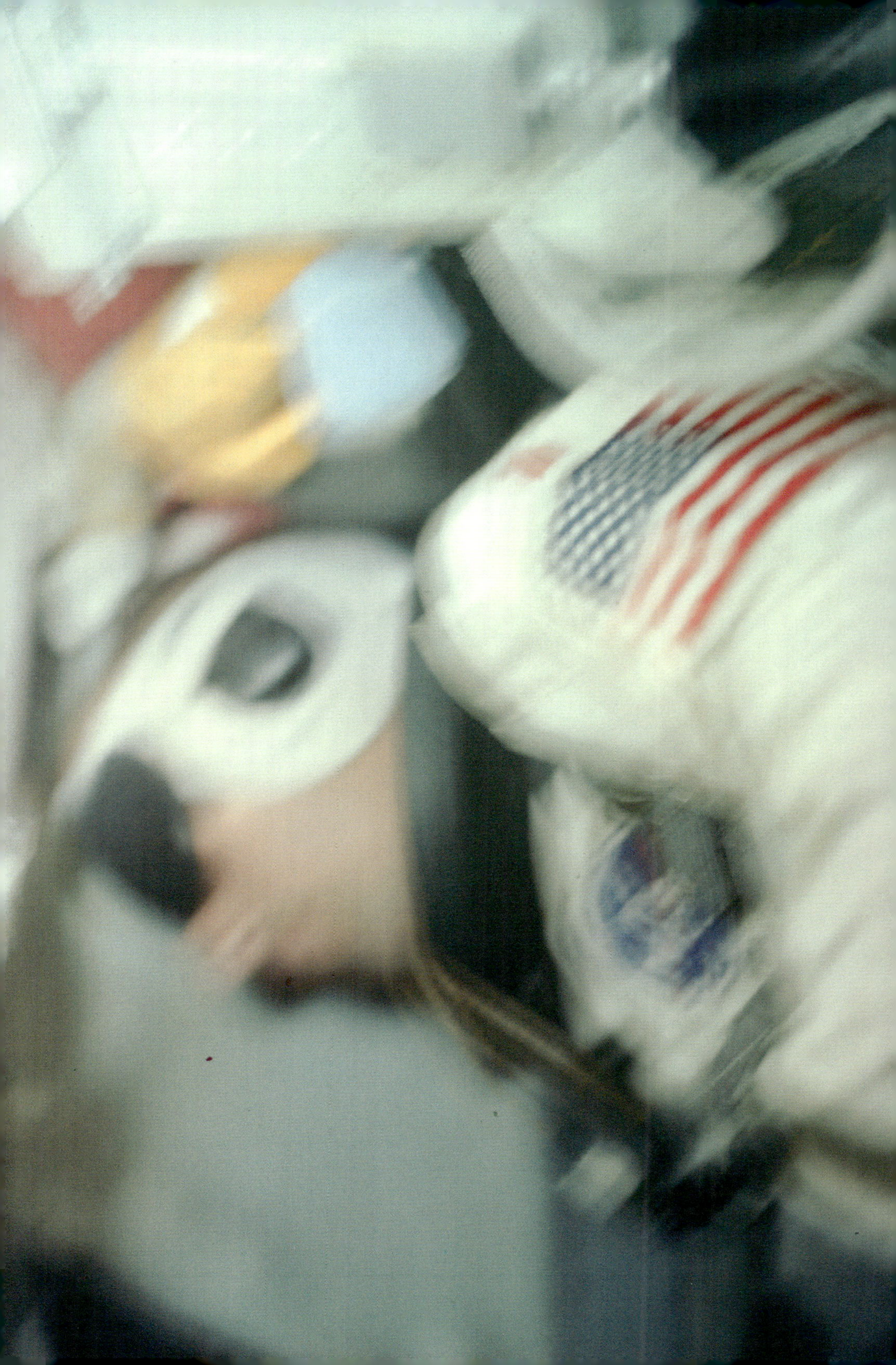

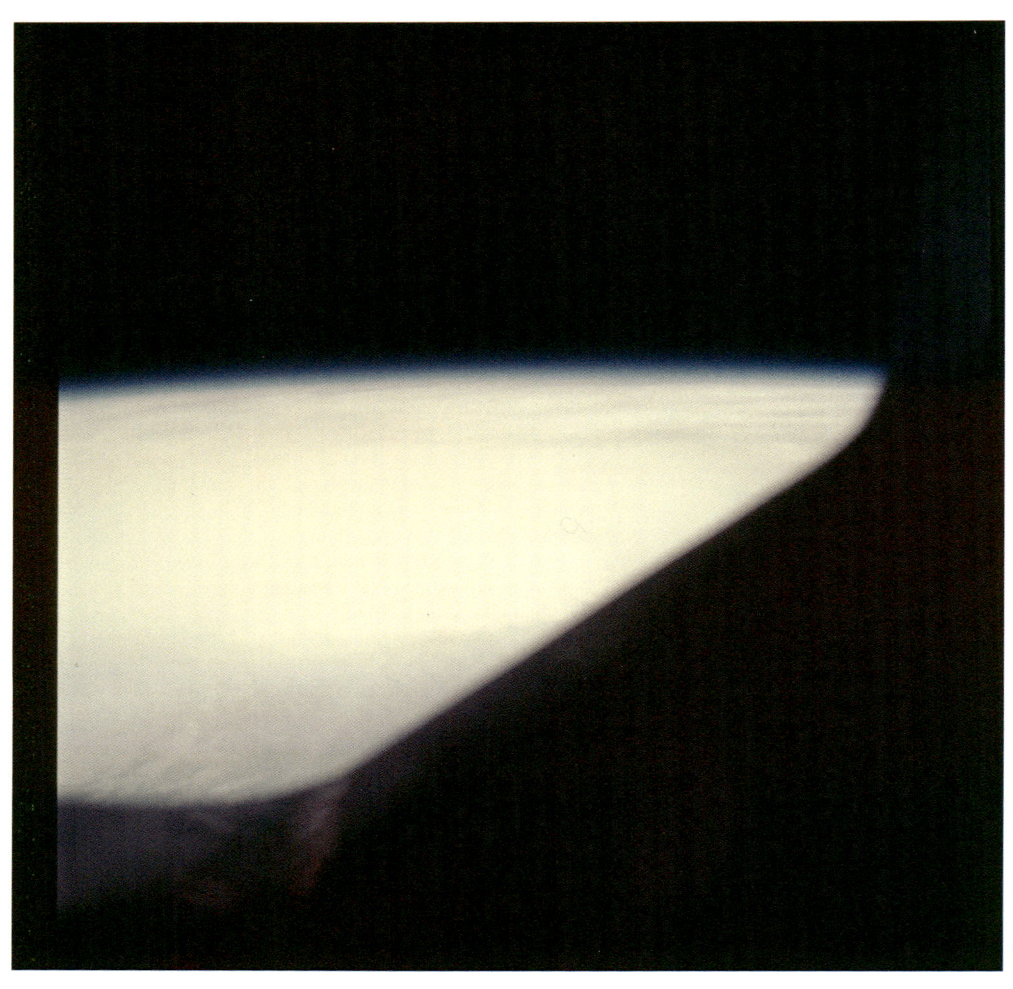

Apollo 7, October 11, 1968

*Gulf of Mexico. Very high oblique. Cloud Cover
100%.* Hasselblad 500C (70mm); Zeiss Planar
80mm f/2.8 lens; Kodak Ektachrome SO-121
High Resolution Aerial Color Film.

Gemini 7, December 17, 1965

Chad: southeast of Lake Chad taken during orbit number 190. Hasselblad 500C (70mm); Zeiss Planar 80mm f/2.8 lens; Kodak Ektachrome SO-217 Medium Speed ASA 64 Color Reversal Film.

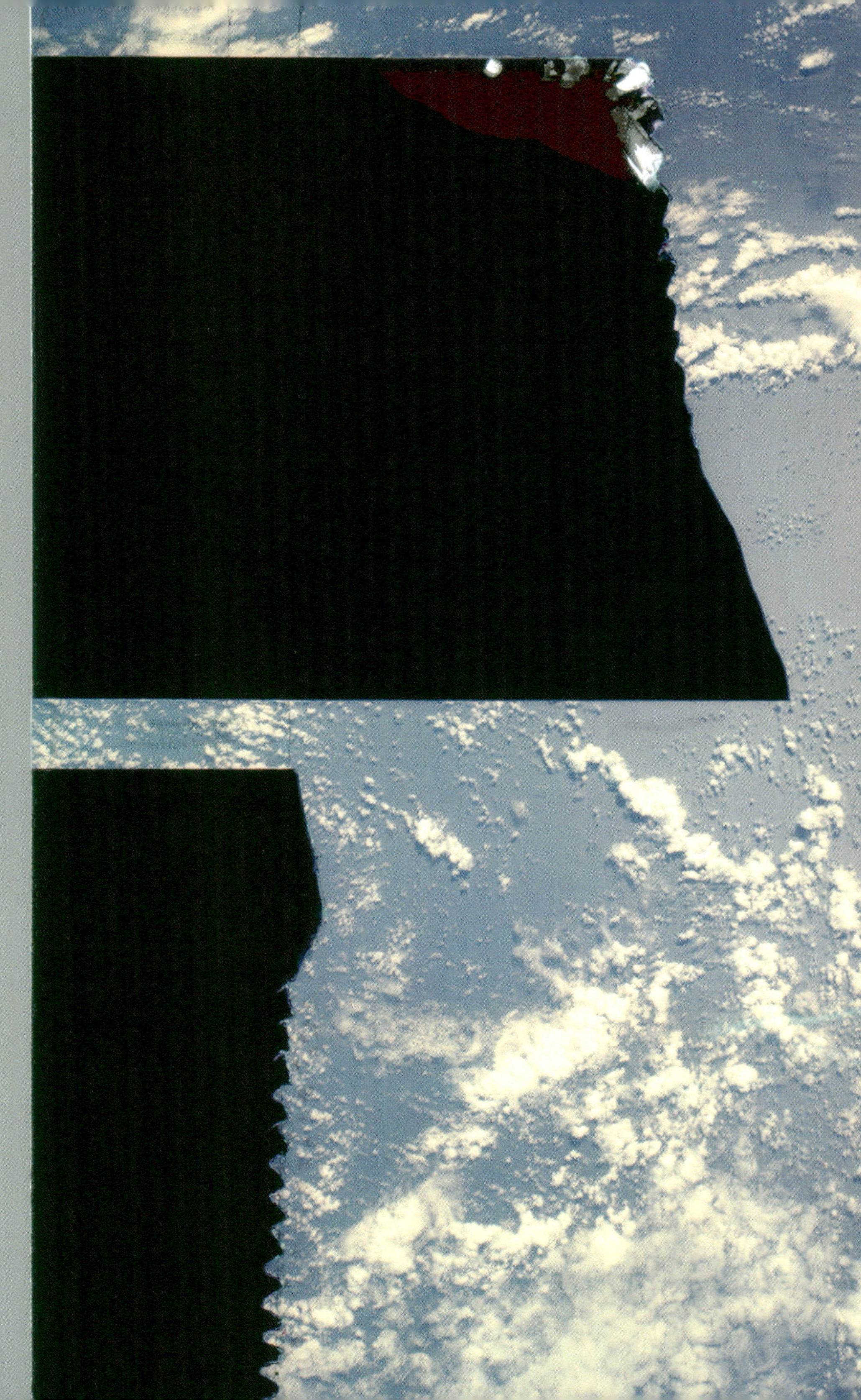

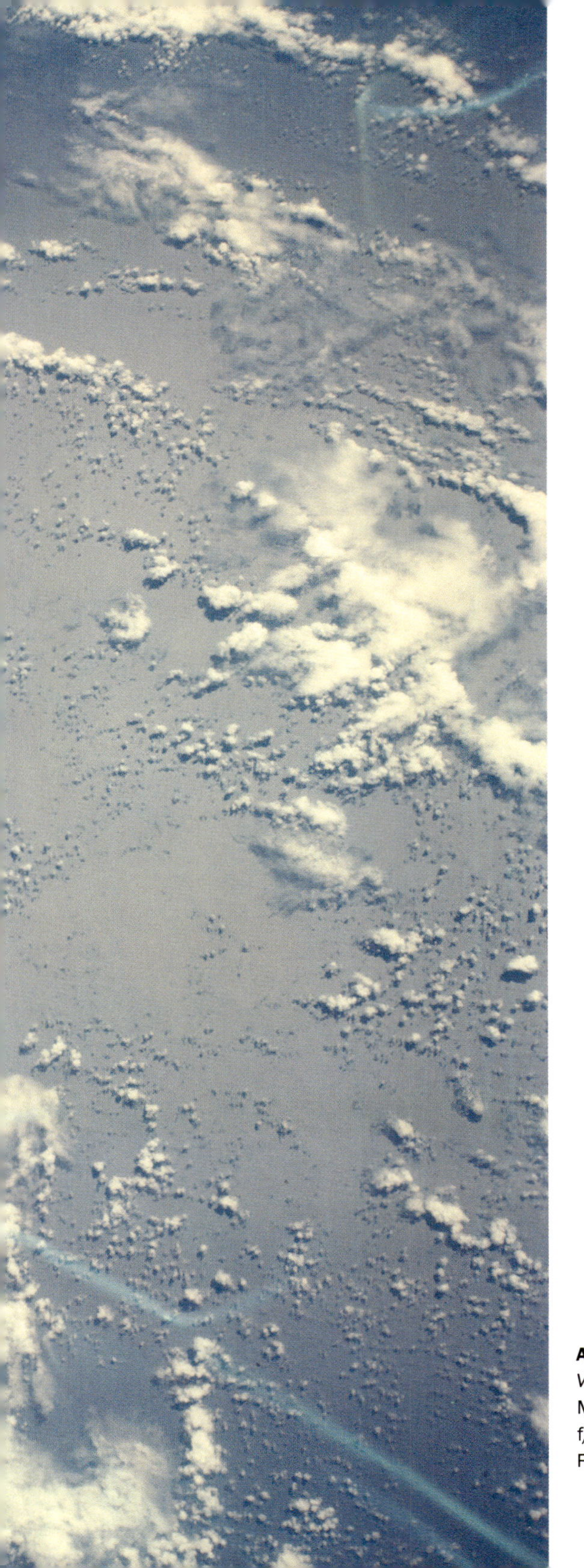

Apollo 6, April 4, 1968
View taken over the Atlantic Ocean. J. A.
Maurer 220G (70mm); Kodak Ektar 76mm
f/2.8 lens; Kodak Ektachrome SO-121 High
Resolution Aerial ASA 64 color Film.

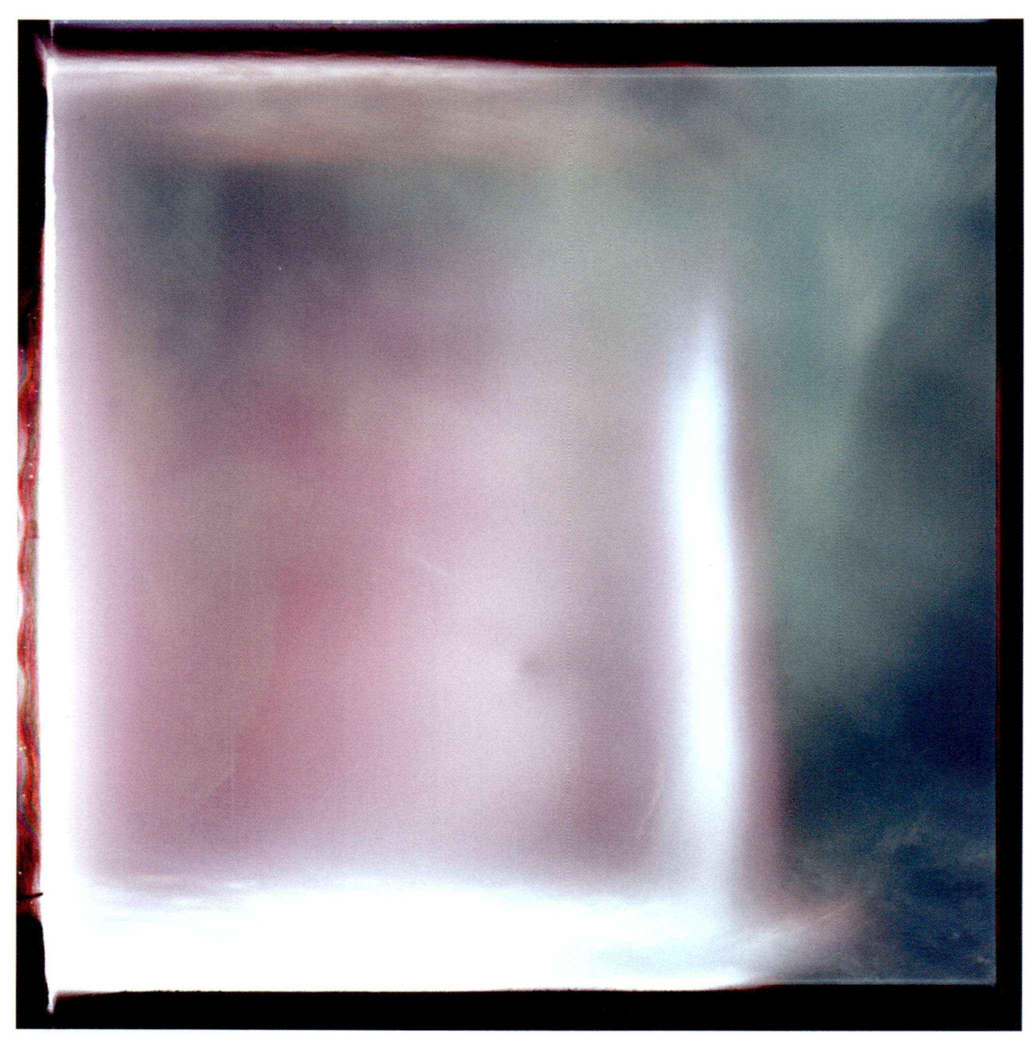

Gemini 7, December 17, 1965
Overexposed and out of focus. Hasselblad
500C (70mm); Zeiss Planar 80mm f/2.8 lens;
Kodak Ektachrome SO-217 Medium Speed
ASA 64 Color Reversal Film.

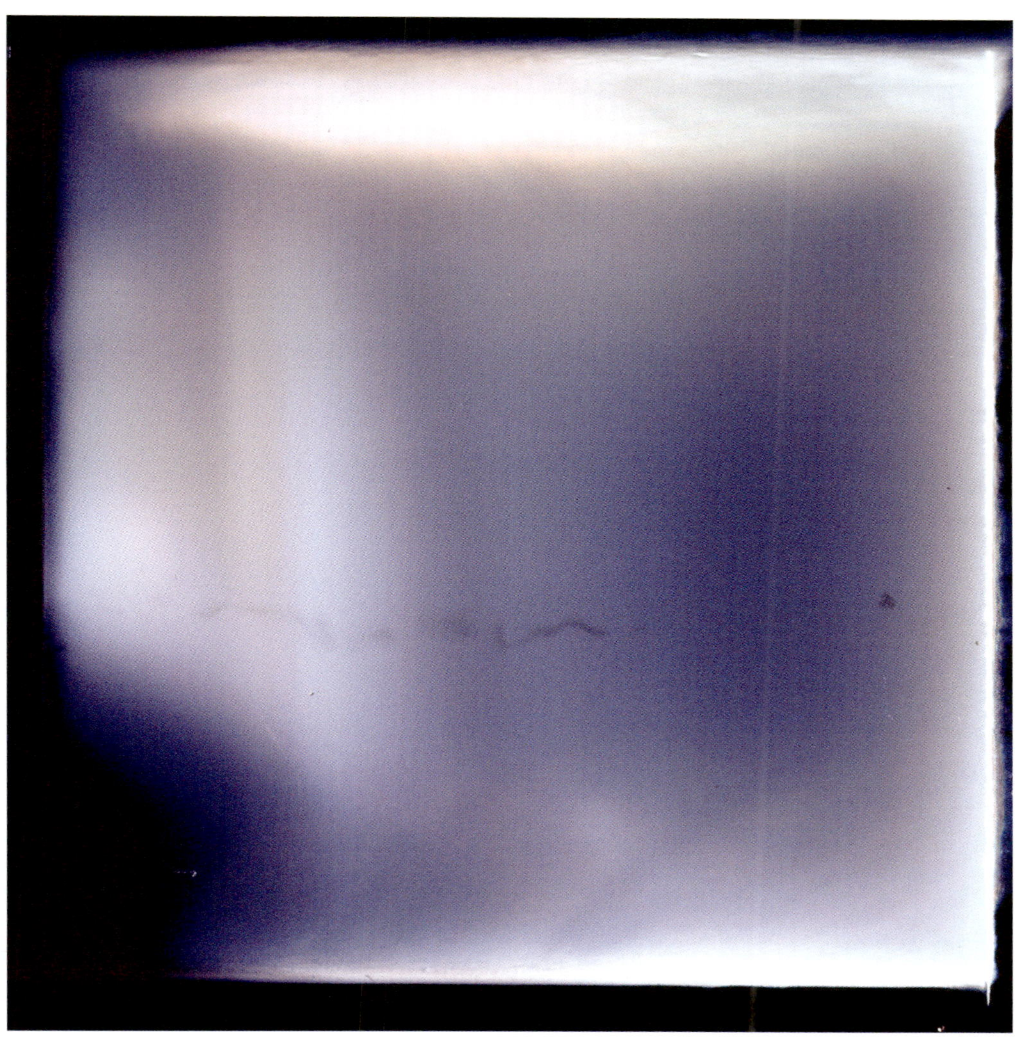

Gemini 7, December 12, 1965
Overexposed. Hasselblad 500C (70mm);
Zeiss Planar 80mm f/2.8 lens; Kodak Ekta-
chrome SO-217 Medium Speed ASA 64 Color
Reversal Film.

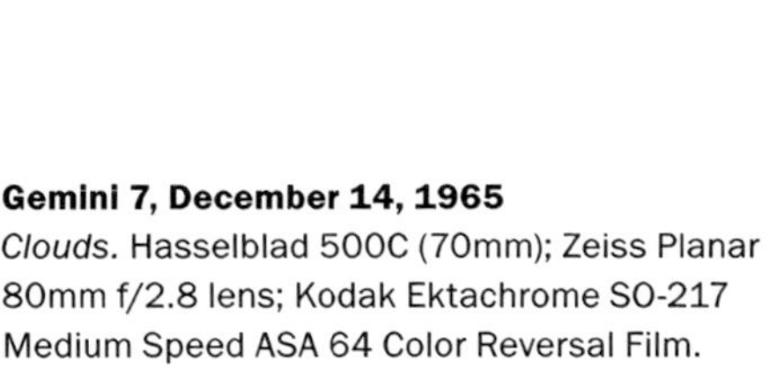

Gemini 7, December 14, 1965
Clouds. Hasselblad 500C (70mm); Zeiss Planar
80mm f/2.8 lens; Kodak Ektachrome SO-217
Medium Speed ASA 64 Color Reversal Film.

Apollo 16, April 25, 1972
View of Station Lunar Module taken during the third Extravehicular Activity. Hasselblad 500EL Data Camera (70mm); Zeiss Biogon 60mm f/5.6 lens; Kodak Ektachrome SO-168 EF High Speed ASA 160 Color Reversal Film.

Gemini 9, June 6, 1966
Partial frame of Ethiopia-Somali-French Somali: Land Gulf of Aden taken during orbit number 43. Maurer Space Camera (70mm); Schneider Xenotar 80mm f/2.8 lens; Kodak Ektachrome SO-217 Medium Speed ASA 64 Color Reversal Film.

Apollo 12, November 18, 1969

Washed out. Hasselblad 500EL Data Camera
(70mm); Zeiss Biogon 60mm f/5.6 lens; Kodak
SO-267 Plus-XX High Speed ASA 278 Black
and White Film.

Apollo 12, November 16, 1969
Not plottable. Hasselblad 500EL (70mm);
Zeiss Sonnar 250mm f/5.6 lens; Kodak
SO-164 Medium Speed AEI 20 Black and
White Film.

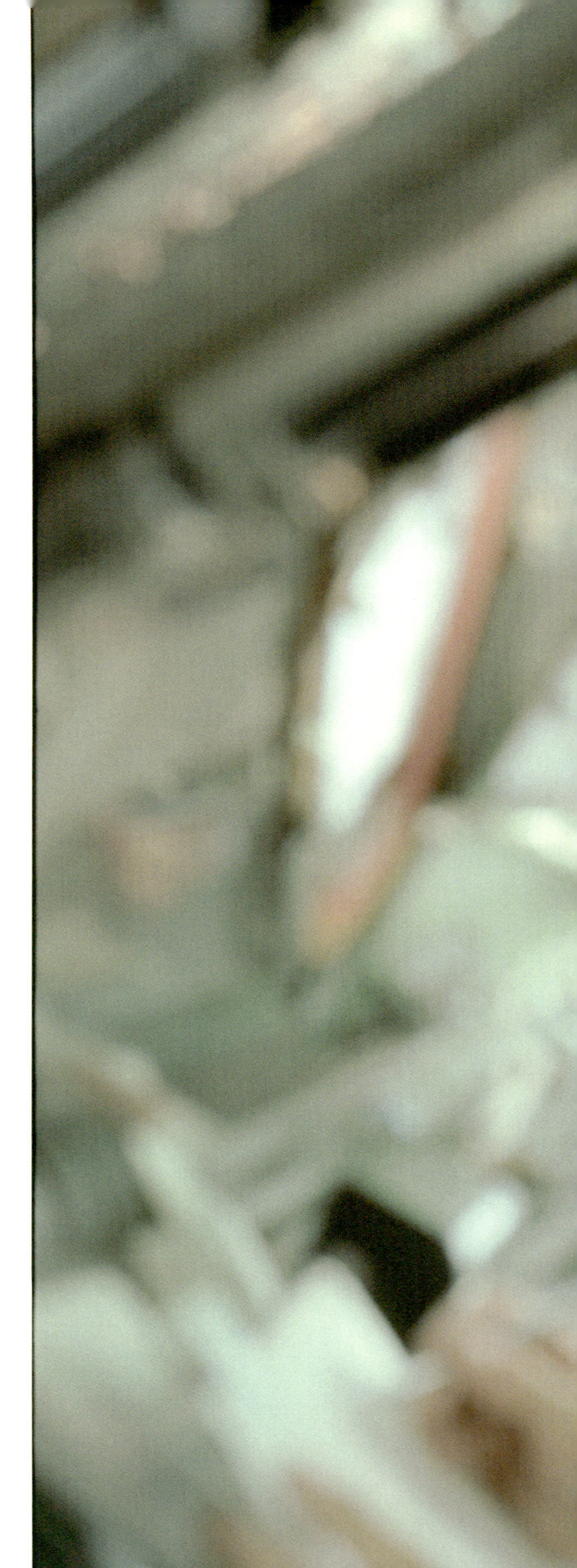

Apollo 7, October 11, 1968
Astronaut working inside the Command Module. Hasselblad 500C (70mm); Zeiss Planar 80mm f/2.8 lens; Kodak Ektachrome SO-368 Medium Speed ASA 64 Color Reversal Film.

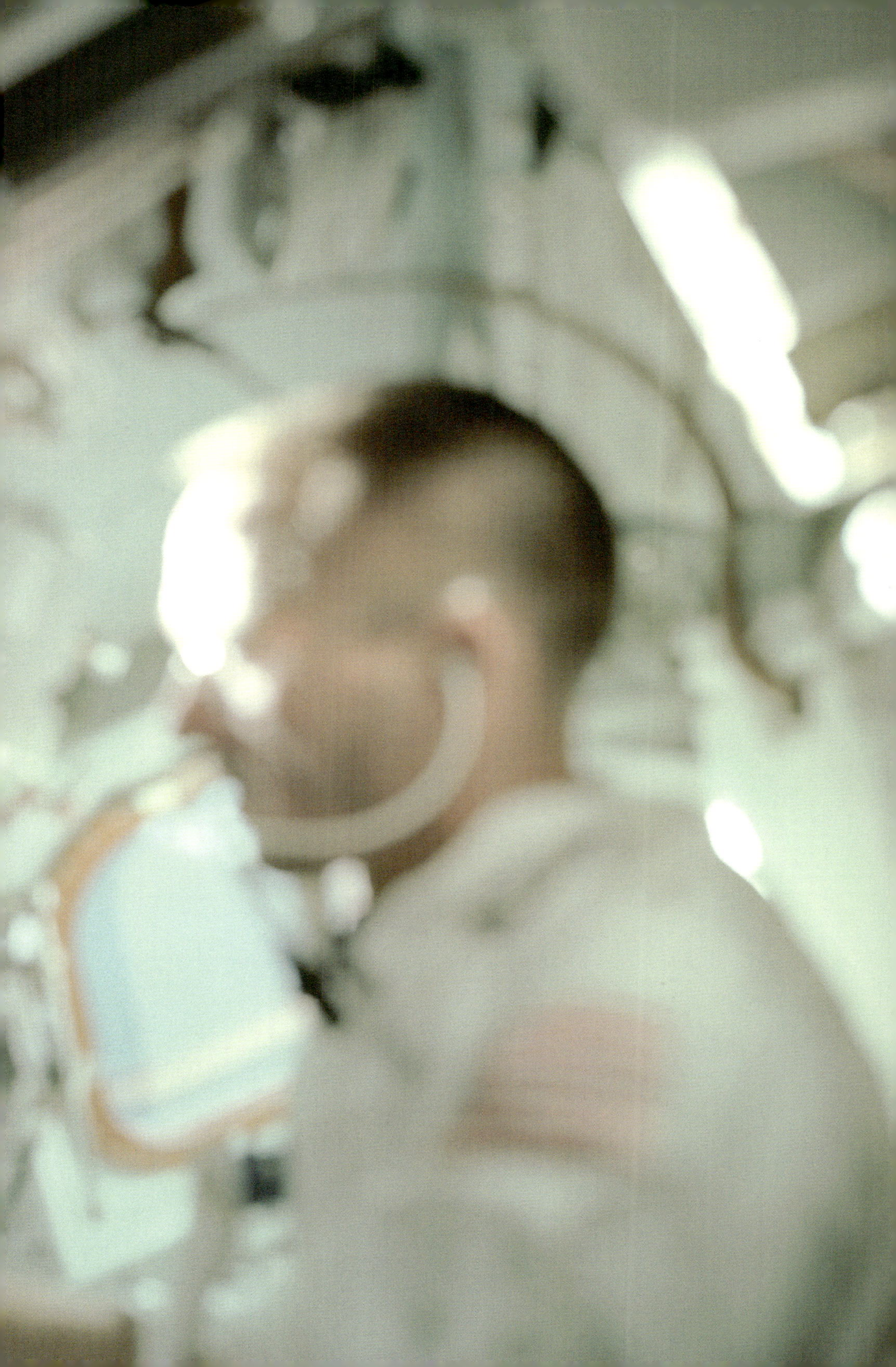

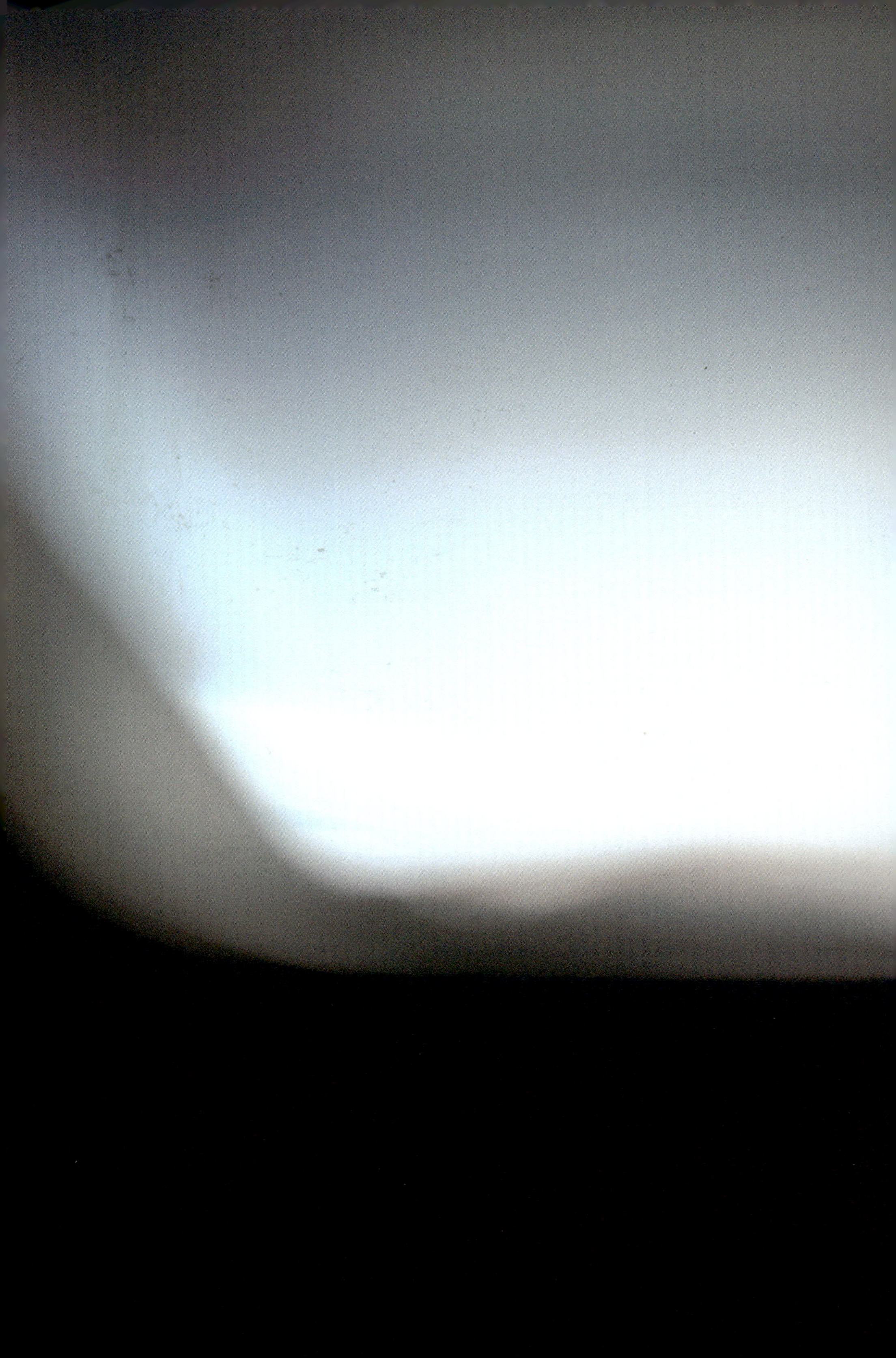

Mercury-Atlas 6, February 20, 1962
Unclear. Ansco Autoset (35mm); Fixed 50mm
f/2.8 lens; Eastman Color Negative Film 5250.

Mercury-Atlas 8, October 3, 1962
Blurred Earth view. Hasselblad 500C (70mm);
Zeiss Planar 80mm f/2.8 lens; GAF Super
Anscochrome D-200 Color Reversal Film.

Apollo 10, May 24, 1969

Oblique view of Sinus Medii. Longitude was 1.5 degrees east and Latitude was 1.5 degrees north. Sun angle was low. Hasselblad 500EL (70mm); Zeiss Planar 80mm f/2.8 lens; Kodak Ektachrome 3400 Panatomic-X Aerial ASA 80 Black and White Film.

Apollo 7, October 12, 1968
Overexposed image. Hasselblad 500C
(70mm); Zeiss Planar 80mm f/2.8 lens; Kodak
Ektachrome 3400 Panatomic-X Aerial ASA 80
Black and White Film.

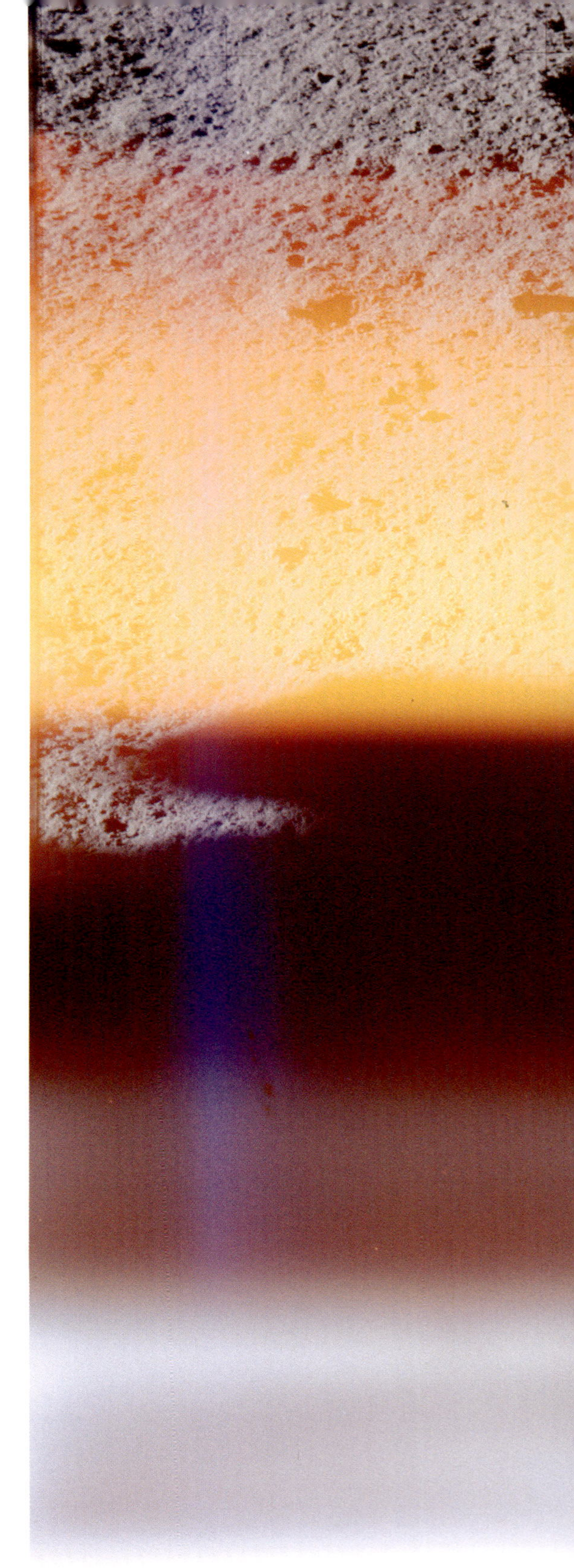

Apollo 15, July 30, 1971
View of Station 1 and Sample 156, down sun
taken during the first Extravehicular Activity.
Hasselblad 500EL Data Camera (70mm);
Zeiss Biogon 60mm f/5.6 lens; Kodak Ekta-
chrome SO-168 EF High Speed ASA 160 Color
Reversal Film.

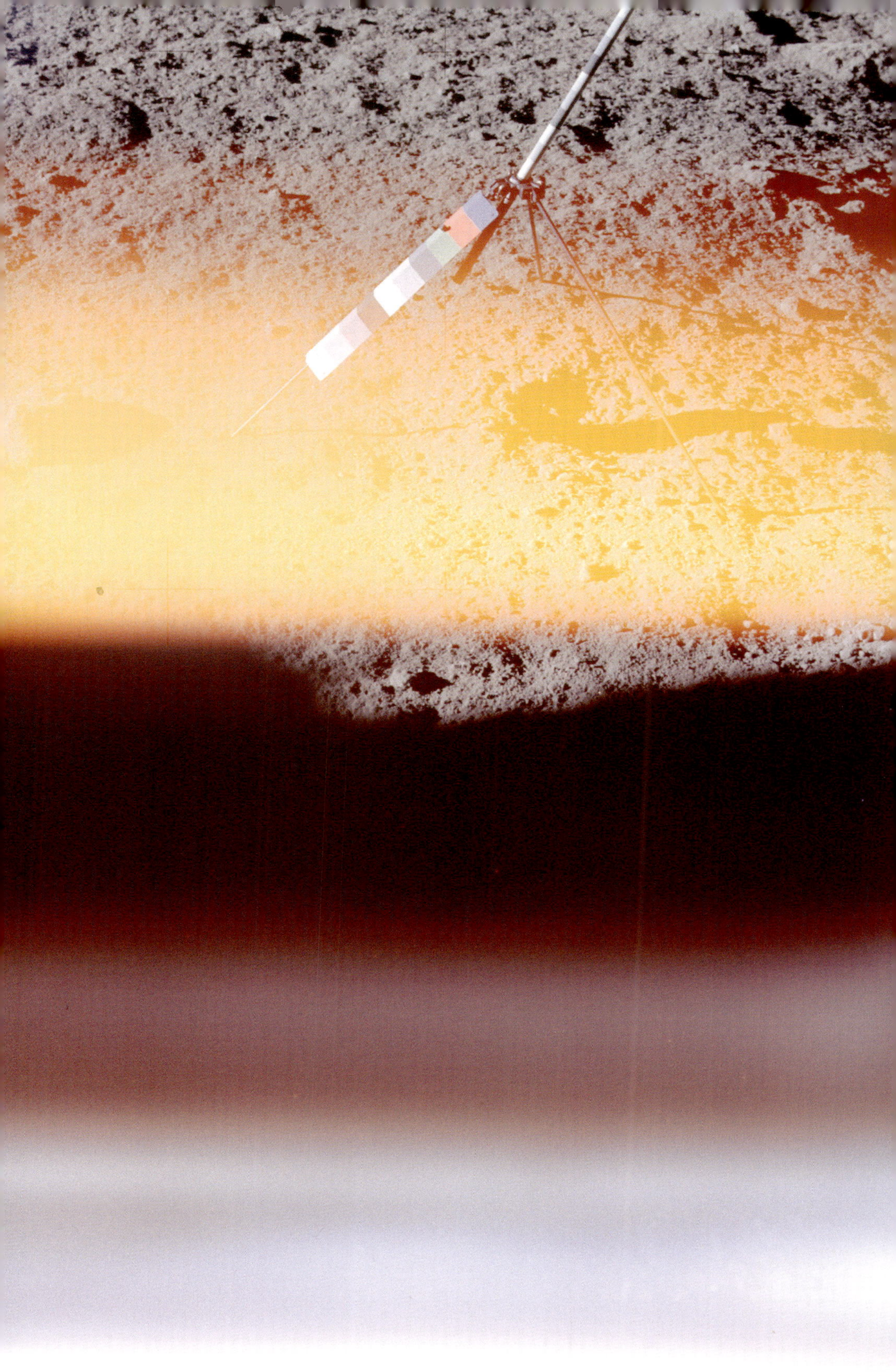

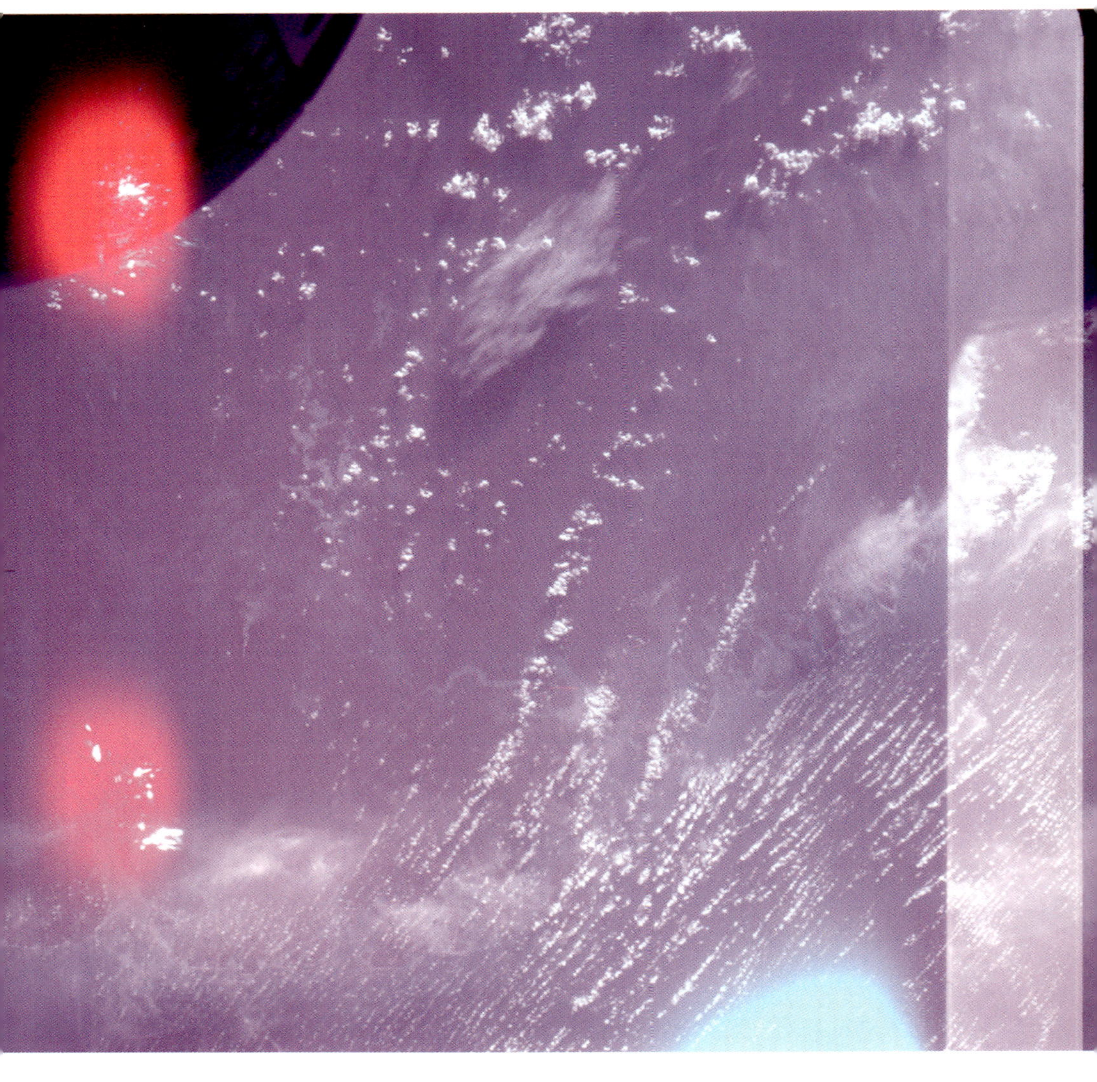

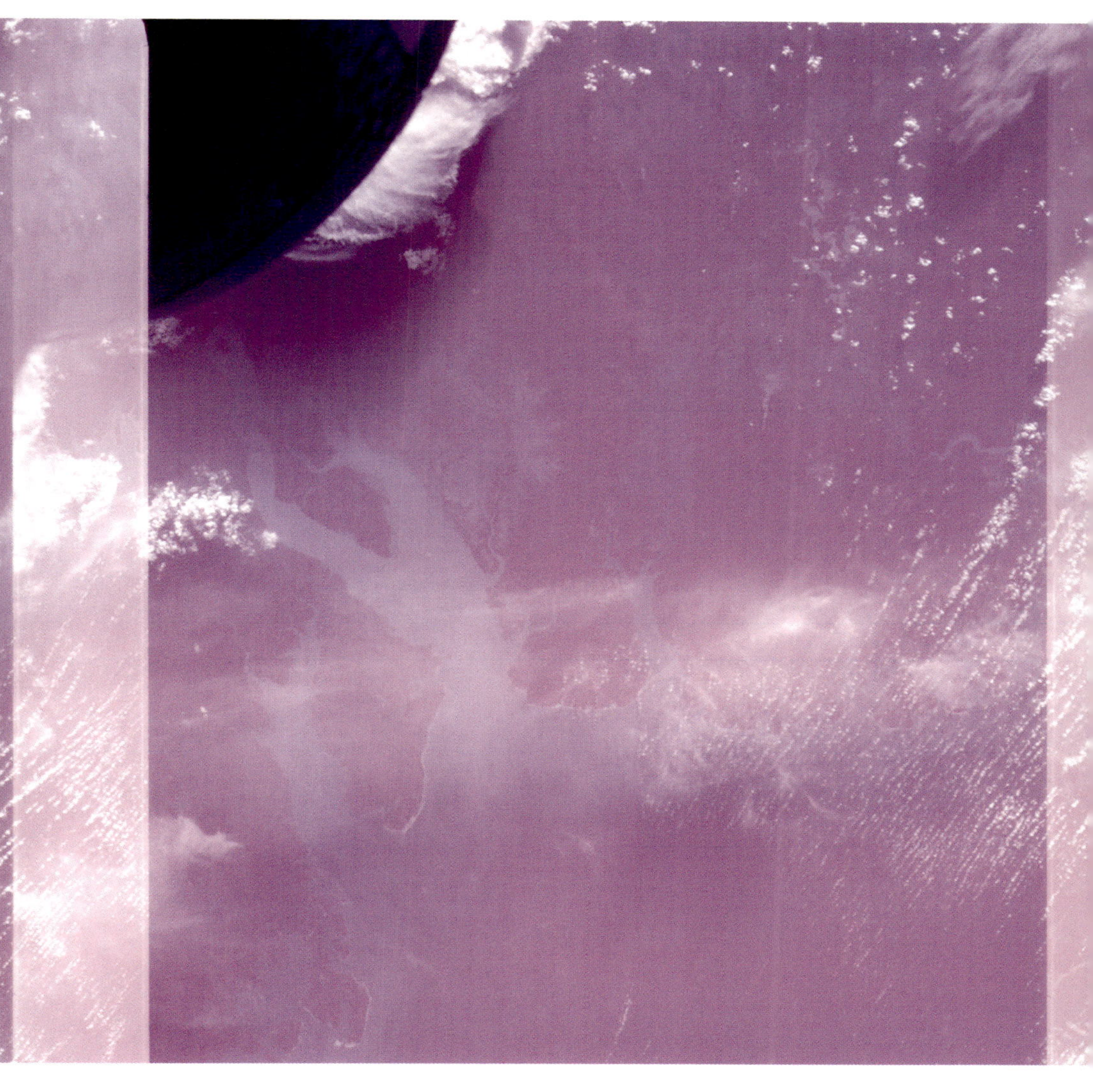

Gemini 7, December 9, 1965

Brazil: Para and Maranhao States; Atlantic Ocean (no filter) taken during orbit number 121. Hasselblad 500C (70mm); Zeiss Planar 80mm f/2.8 lens; Kodak Ektachrome 8443 Infrared Aerial Color Film.

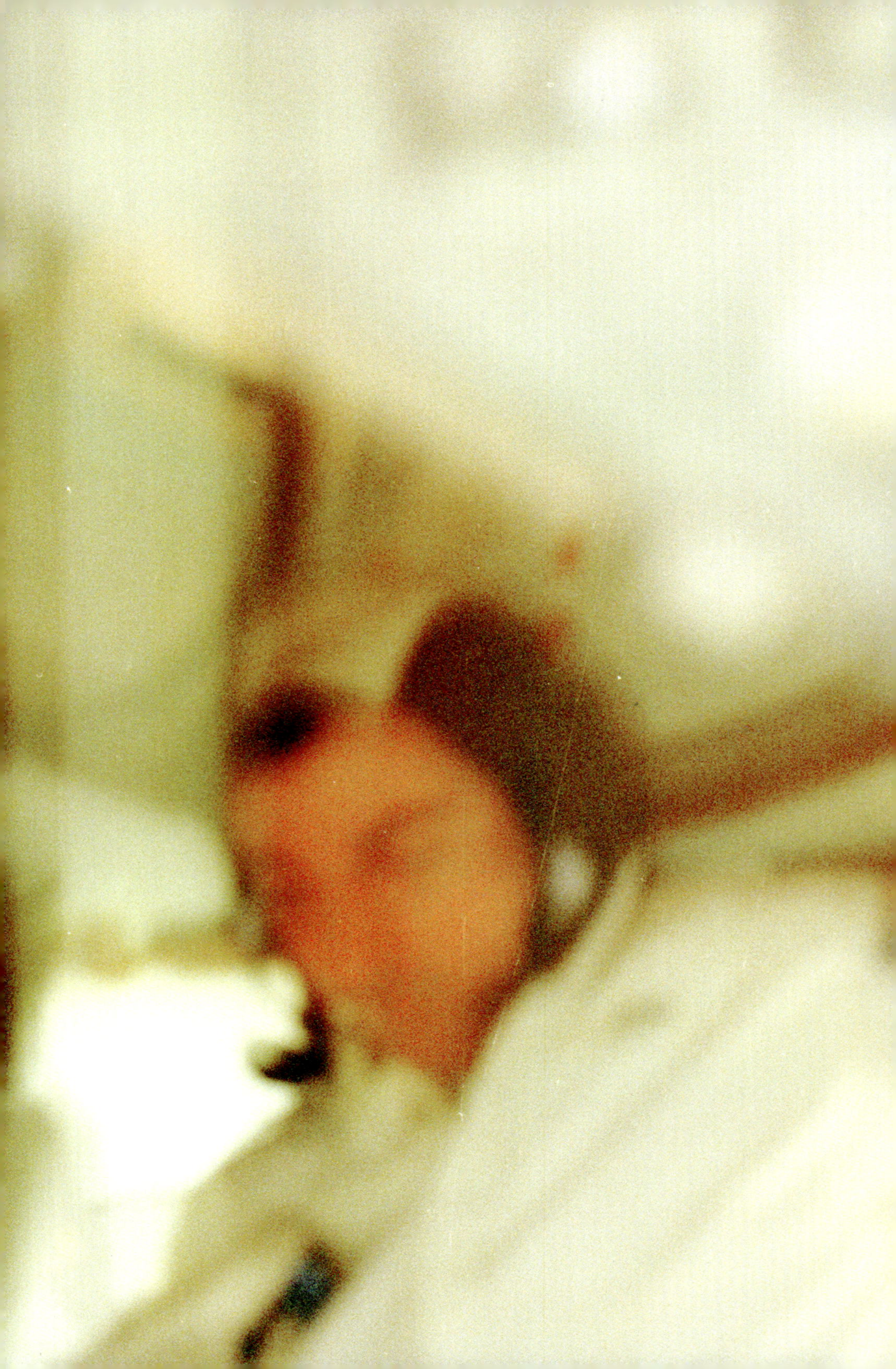

Apollo 10, May 24, 1969
Hasselblad 500EL (70mm); 70mm lens; Kodak
Ektachrome SO-368 medium speed ASA 64
Color Reversal Film.

FOLLOWING SPREAD
Apollo 16, April 18, 1972
*View of Station 9 and the front of the Lunar
Roving Vehicle taken during the second
Extravehicular Activity.* Hasselblad 500EL
Data Camera (70mm); Zeiss Biogon 60mm
f/5.6 lens; Kodak Ektachrome SO-168 EF High
Speed ASA 160 Color Reversal Film.

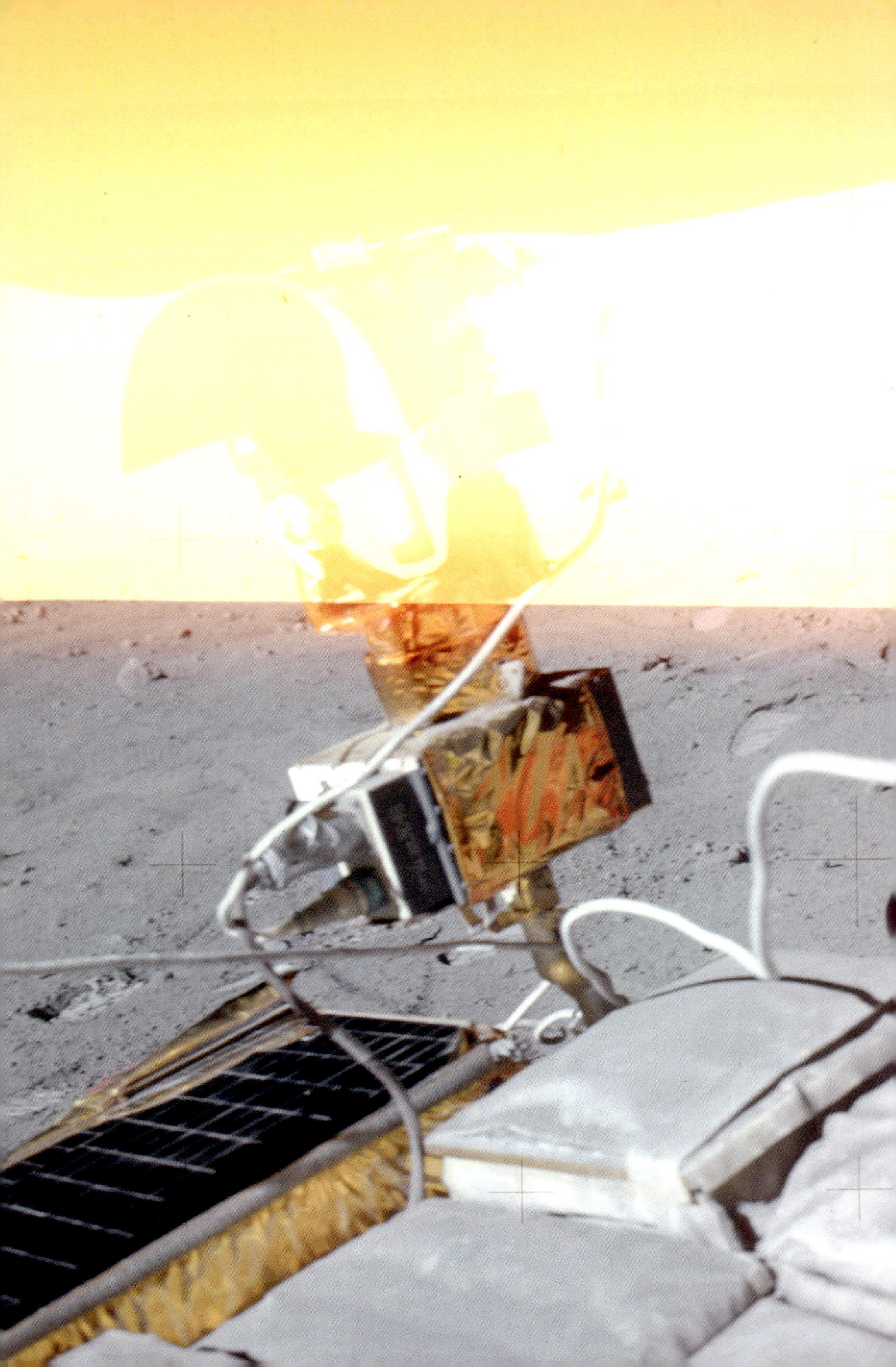

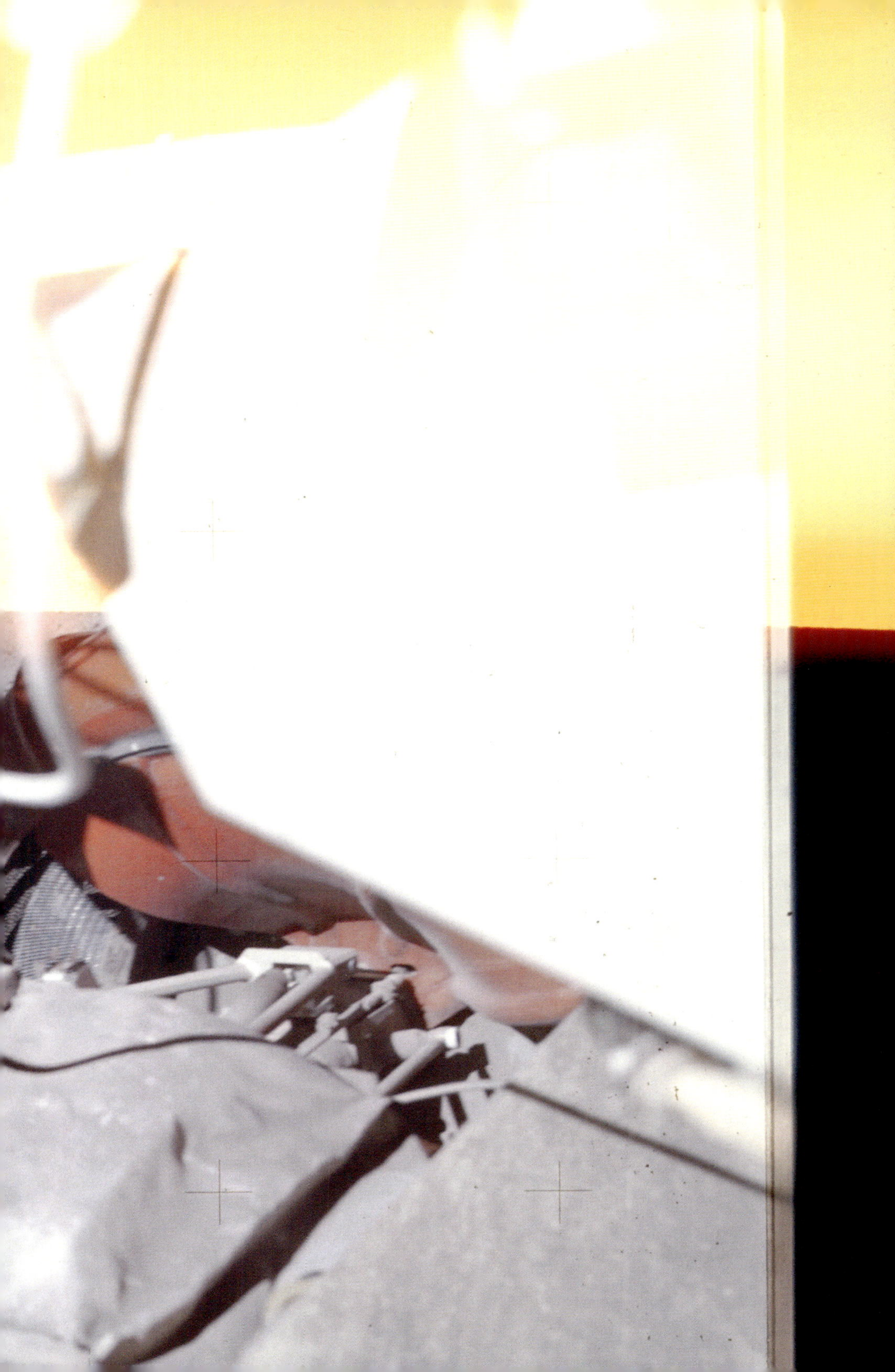

Like Nothing on Earth: Photographic Artifacts from Early NASA Missions

The National Archives, established in 1934, is the official record keeper of the U.S. government. By law, federal records with long-term value are sent to the Archives. These records are preserved indefinitely to ensure access and accountability. Sincere gratitude for their work.

Paul Morgan is a California visual artist.

A Current Editions publication

Current Editions LLC
Emeryville, California

hi@currenteditions.biz
www.currenteditions.biz

We research, design, and publish assorted ephemera. It is a project of Jessalyn Aaland and Paul Morgan.

Current Editions No. 12

Copy editing by Jessalyn Aaland

Designed by Paul Morgan
Typeset in Century Schoolbook and Franklin Gothic

Printed in California

ISBN 979-8-9992256-0-3

First edition
Printing of 500
June 2025

Captions were compiled from official NASA archives, including mission transcripts, press releases, and historical documentation. These records reflected the language and formatting conventions of their time, so adjustments were made to standardize spelling, capitalization, and formatting. Edits were intended to enhance readability and consistency.

FRONT COVER

Apollo 15, August 2, 1971

View of the Lunar Disc with Seas of Crises (Mare Crisium), Fertility (Mare Fecunditatis), Serenity (Mare Serenitatis) and Smyth's Sea (Mare Smythii) visible. Image was taken during the Trans-Earth Coast period. Hasselblad 500EL Data Camera (70mm); Zeiss Biogon 60mm f/5.6 lens; Kodak Ektachrome SO-168 EF high speed ASA 160 Color Reversal Film.

BACK COVER

Apollo 7, November 19, 1969

Color chart on the lunar surface. A panel from the Solar Wind Composition Experiment is visible in the background. Image was taken during the second Extravehicular Activity. Hasselblad 500EL Data Camera (70mm); Zeiss Biogon 60mm f/5.6 lens; Kodak SO-267 Plus-XX High-Speed ASA 278 Black and White Film.

FRONTISPIECE

Mercury-Redstone 2, January 31, 1961

Earth observation. The flight number and a mag or frame number are visible at the top right and center of the photo. A clock face is visible in the top left of the photo. J. A. Maurer 220G (70mm); General Scientific Finitar 75mm f/2.8 lens; GAF Super Anscochrome T-100 Superior ASA 64 Color Reversal Film.